Shadow Warriors Training Manual

By Jamie Seal

Printed in the United Kingdom
First Printing, 2022
ISBN 9798805498078

Website: www.sealmartialarts.co.uk
Email: info@sealmartialarts.co.uk
Facebook : www.facebook.com/SealMartialArts/

"Nobody can perform a move perfectly on the first attempt, Keep training and you'll master the art"

Jamie Seal

Grading and Belt Rank Structure

Black Belt - 1st Dan -

Brown Belt With Black Stripe – 1st kyu -

Brown Belt – 2nd kyu -

Purple Belt – 3rd Kyu -

Blue Belt – 4th kyu -

Green Belt – 5th kyu -

Orange Belt With Black Stripe –
6th Kyu -

Orange belt – 7th kyu -

Yellow Belt - 8th Kyu -

Red Belt – 9th Kyu -

10 Things To Help You Improve Your Ninjutsu

1. Practice at least 30 minutes a week at home.

2. The things you enjoy least are the things you need to practice more.

3. Eat healthily, It helps your body and mind to stay strong.

4. Set some goals and achievements.

5. Keep your uniform clean and tidy, It helps you focus.

6. To not do too much, rest is important too.

7. Show your friends and family, Be proud.

8. Read up on what you do, It will help you during lessons.

9. Visualise yourself doing well.

10. Look to improve one thing at a time.

<u>Seal Martial Arts Dojo Rules</u>

1. Respect your training partners.
They are here to learn just like you. They trust you not to hurt them but to help them. If you wish to carry out a technique correctly you must allow them to do so to you as well.

2. Respect the dojo.
This where you train and where you learn - not just the art of the ninja but about yourself. You bow when stepping onto the mat at the start of training and bow when stepping off at the end. This is a place of learning that requires your focus and attention.

3. Listen to the Sensei.
The person teaching the class is Sensei. You should address them as Sensei and listen when they are explaining points in class. The Sensei will always try to help you learn, but you must apply yourself for this to happen. You must always ask for help if you have difficulty understanding anything.

4. Stay focused throughout the class.
You must keep your focus from the moment you step onto the mat to the moment you leave at the end of the class. This means you do not talk about events outside of class, you are quiet when you are spoken to, and concentrate on every aspect of your training. Disruptive students will be sat out of the class for some or all of the lesson.

5. Dress to train.
We practice a Japanese art. You will therefore be dressed in gi trousers and jacket, with your belt correctly tied. If you ask, you may wear the dojo t shirt instead of the gi jacket, but the belt will still be worn with this. There will be no other t shirts worn.

6. Do not misbehave with training equipment.

You will at times use equipment to train, be it crash mats, vaulting box, or weapons. You will respect these and carry out the exercises and techniques as directed. Any inappropriate behaviour will result in the student sitting out a part of the class. Continued misbehaviour will result in the student sitting out for the remainder of that class.

7. Ask if you need to leave the mat.

If you need water, a toilet break, or need to stop training for any reason you will ask Sensei first so they know why you are not training. This is so they are aware of where you are for safety reasons.

8. Gradings will be every 3 months.

From January 2019 gradings will start being regular every 3 months. If you are due a grading you will be told one month in advance and reminded the week before. Not everyone will grade at the same time. If you are not graded after 6 months you will be told why and what you need to improve on. Poor or inappropriate behaviour will delay any grading.

9. Help others to improve yourself.

You need to help each other in training. The higher grades always have the responsibility to help the most. This means you are polite, there is no name calling or insults. You will learn more by helping than by hurting, this will be watched for even closer when it comes near to your grading time.

10. Report accidents and worries

If you see another student get hurt during training or you are worried for their safety you must report in to the instructor as soon as possible. It is important that student are safe when training. Always ask the Sensei if you need to leave the room.

How We Train

When we train in ninjutsu we are learning how to move correctly, how to be aware of our surroundings at all times and how to meet aggression without anger, without fear and without hate.

We must be able to remain calm in the eye of the storm, letting it pass us by if we can, avoiding injury if we cannot, and only using ninjutsu skills learned if we have no other option, and then only to escape injury not to inflict it.

When we train in the dojo we treat our training partner with respect, we adapt the amount of force applied in each technique to a level where it is effective but where it does not injure our training partner.

We listen to our training partner and work with them to improve and develop in ninjutsu. Only when the student is seen to be able to control themselves with their techniques will they advance to train with another student.

Weapons will only be taught under direct supervision of the instructors. Weapons must be treated with respect, any student seen to be using weapons in a manner that is considered dangerous will be taken out of that class.

Ninjutsu Philosophy

The main philosophy behind ninjutsu can be said one of avoiding conflict. The *Nin* of ninjutsu means enduring or surviving.

In the era of the ninja clans of Japan their land was in a state of constant warfare. The only way they could protect their families was to work behind the scenes to find an unconventional way to survive.

They developed many methods of being unnoticed, becoming almost invisible, and found ways to influence the decision makers of that era.

From this art we use all the methods of becoming unnoticed by aggressors, of surviving conflict, of finding a solution that takes confrontation away from the fight to one of winning.

Above all ninjutsu is the art of winning.

In an ideal world this would be always possible but sometimes there is no room for us to win without physical confrontation and the art of ninjutsu provides a whole variety of responses to allow us to control the fight, to escape unharmed and to end it quickly and effectively.

All junior students are advised that if at any time they are suspected of using what they are taught to bully, intimidate or start fights they will be suspended from training until their parent(s) are happy for them to continue and that their instructor has assurances from the student that such behaviour has stopped.

Parents and students are all welcome to discuss with the instructors any concerns they may have either before or after the lesson or to contact us at any other time.

9

Where To Start

Appearance
The Ninjutsu student should dress in uniform, never show up in wrinkled or dirty clothing. The student must learn to tie their own belt for their first rank promotion, 9th Kyu (red belt). This will be shown in class.

Warm up
It is important to warm your muscles before beginning any exercise or stretching. Here are some things you can do to warm up:

Jog around the edge of the mats in the dojo 5 times.
Shi Ho Tenchi Tobi - Leaping in 4 directions.
Practice the Sanshin No Kata - 5 Elemental Forms.
Plank for 30 seconds (Zenpo Ukemi)
Small Circles (Draw small circles with your hands for 30 secs)
High and low blocks
Taihenjutsu dodge ball (Avoid with rolls and break falls)
Sensei says (Sensei says Ichimonji No Kamae)
Taisabaki twister (Colours on the floor, working on footwork)
Warm up with foam Nunchaku (1 minute of passing)
Bo Furi Gata with foam Bo/Jo staff (Staff spinning)

Breathing Exercises

Frontal Breathing - Shomen Kokyuho
Assume the Seiza position.
Pull back both shoulders opening the shoulders and chest, inhale.
As you drop both shoulders forward and round the back, exhale completely. Perform this eight times slowly.

Left and Right Deep Breathing - Seiza Sayu Shinkokyu
Assume the Seiza position.
Turn to face the right, pull back the right shoulder, inhale.
Dropping the right shoulder, turn back to the front, exhale completely.
Likewise inhale turn to the left then exhale completely return to face forwards. Perform this eight times slowly.

Extension Deep Breathing - Shinten Shinkokyu
From a position of sitting on the ground.
Stretch out the hands and feet directly to the front
From this four limb extended seat, spread the hands & arms widely and breathe in deeply
Close the arms and hands as if to put them forward on top of the legs, exhale completely.
Perform this eight times slowly.

Stretching - **Junan Taiso**

Every day you should stretch your large muscles.
Perform the following exercises as you have seen them in class.

10 times each.

Standing Stretches

1. Neck rotations
2. Wrist bends
3. Shoulder rotations and stretches
4. Bend at the waist and do large circles
5. Hip rotations
6. Knee rotations

Sitting Stretches

1. Ankle rotations
2. Toes back and forth
3. Tuck in leg, stretch to long leg (hold for 10 seconds)
4. Legs apart, stretch to right and left and centre
(hold for 10 seconds)
5. Straight legs in front stretch (hold for 10 seconds breathe, don't hold your breath when stretching)
6. Bottoms of feet together, down to centre (hold for 10 seconds)
7. Quadricep stretches
8. Cat stretches

Partner Stretching:

If you have a friend to help you, you can become limber quickly.

1. Stand holding onto a wall or chair back. Turn your leg closest to the wall towards the wall, lift your other leg out to the side and let your partner lift it while you push against their lift. Tell them when to stop and count to 10 slowly.

Repeat but lift leg forward.

Perform on both legs and both people.

2. Sit facing each other and stretch out legs in front. Push your feet bottoms against the inside of the thighs of your partner. Hold hands and pull them forward so their face goes to the floor. Hold and count to 10 slowly. Repeat with other person's legs inside and other person pulling.

Stances - Kamae

KAMAE NO KATA

Kamae are the stances we move through when using Taijutsu (body movement) to defend ourselves. They should not be used as static poses to be assumed when threatened but should be moved into when attacked to respond with the right technique.

The techniques that will be learnt may well start from some of these Kamae, but this is for training in body movement while in the dojo and will be explained more in depth where appropriate in the lessons.

Start by trying to remember the Kamae No Kata above.

Full Body Movement - Taihenjutsu

This is the art of rebounding from the ground, where the student learns how to roll in any direction no matter the circumstances and still observe the opponent.

Falling Forms - Ukemi Gata

Forward Techniques - Mae Gaeshi

Forward Roll / Passive Defence - Zenpo Kaiten
Two-Handed Roll - Zenpo Kaiten Ryote
One-Handed Roll - Zenpo Kaiten Katate
No Handed Roll - Zenpo Kaiten Mute

Forward Break Fall - Mae Ukemi / Zenpo Ukemi - With both hands from standing or kneeling with a Koho Geri (Back Kick).

Sideways Techniques - Yoko Gaeshi

Sideways Roll - Sokuho Kaiten
Sideways Flow - Yoko Nagare
Side Break Fall - Yoko Ukemi

Backwards Techniques - Ushiro Gaeshi

Backwards Roll (short and long) - Koho Kaiten
Backwards Roll With Step (backwards flow) - Ushiro Kaiten
Back Break Fall - Ushiro Ukemi

Reverse Twisting Flow - Gyaku Nagare
Sword Flow - Ken Nagare - Avoiding a cut with a dive roll
Waterfall Drop - Jun Nagare

Leaping in 4 Directions - Shi Ho Ten Chi Tobi
Leaping in four directions (forwards, backwards, left, and right) but not bounding up and down, travelling as far as you can level with the ground using your hips.

High and Low Leaping - Hicho Tobi

Techniques for Climbing to Heaven - Sho Ten No Jutsu
The body's momentum and speed are used for running up vertical obstacles such as trees or walls. Balance training.

Walking Techniques - Ho Ku Jutsu

Ninjutsu Balancing Walk - Shinobi Aruki

Kicking - Keri

When kicking the key point to remember is the knee. Keep your balance low and try to get your knee to your shoulder. Train to have the ability to use your legs and feet naturally, training to kick high (jodan or ten), middle (chudan or shi), and low (gedan or jin).

Forward Stamp Kick - Zenpo Geri
Sideways Stamp Kick - Sokuho Geri
Backwards Stamp Kick - Koho Geri
Heel Kick - Sokuyaku Ken
Ball of Foot Kick - Sokugyaku Ken
Top of Foot Kick - Keri Gaeshi
Jumping Kicks - Tobi Geri
Jumping Front Stamp Kick - Katate Tobi Geri
Kicking With Both Feet - Ryote Tobi Geri

Flying Side Kick - Yoko Tobi Geri
Roundhouse - Mawashi Geri
Low and High Roundhouse - Gedan and Jodan Mawashi Geri
Reverse Roundhouse - Gyaku Mawashi Geri
Side Snap Kick - Yoko Geri
Reverse Side Snap Kick - Gyaku Yoko Geri
Hook Kick - Kagi Geri
Axe Kick - Kakato Geri
360 Crescent Kick - San Hyaku Rokku Ju Mawashi Geri
Checking an Opponents Kick - Sokuyaku Suihei Ken
Sweeping the Leg - Sokuyaku Barai Ken
Heavy Low Leg Kick - Ashi Barai Keri
Natural Kick - Sanshin Keri
Hidden Kick - Kakushi Keri
Kicking To Thighs - Sai Geri
Kicking To Knees - Usai Geri
Knee Strikes - Sokki Ken
Pinning Opponents Foot - Te Dama Dori

8 Ways of Kicking - Happo Geri

1. Right Sokuyaku stamp kick to left thigh
2. Left Sokuyaku stamp kick to right thigh
3. Right swinging inward Sokuyaku to outside of thigh
4. Left swinging inward Sokuyaku to outside of thigh
5. Groin kick by swinging right Sokugyaku (ball of foot) kick up
6. Groin kick by swinging left Sokugyaku (ball of foot) kick up
7. Henka (variations) use a free kicking method to cause pain and force adversary to release grip or back off.
8. Henka (variations) use a free kicking method to cause pain and force adversary to release grip or back off.

<u>Sixteen Striking Fists</u> - Hoken Ju Roppo

Headbutt - Kikaku Ken \ Zu Tsuki - Using the thick bone areas of the forehead, sides, and back of the head in smashing or butting actions.

Elbow Strike - Shuki Ken - Using the bone points of the elbow to strike close targets.

Immovable Fist - Fudo Ken \ Kongo Ken - Using the clenched fist for punching or striking.

Wake Up Rolling Strike / Karate Chop - Kiten Ken \ Shuto - Snapping the hand open at the point of impact, to strike with the outer edge of the palm.

Finger Needle Strike - Shishin Ken - Using any individual fingertips for striking or applying pressure.

Finger Tip Strike - Shitan Ken - Using three or four fingertips together in a stabbing drive.

Claw - Shako Ken - Using the palm and fingers to strike, rake or capture.

Thumb Drive Fist - Shito Ken - Using the extended thumb supported by the clenched fist to strike the target.

Extended Knuckle Fist - Shikan Ken - Using the bones of the middle knuckles of the half folded fingers to strike the target.

Thumb Knuckle Fist - Koppo Ken - Using the middle knuckle of the half folded thumb to strike or apply pressure.

Eight Leaves Strike - Happa Ken - Using the open hand as a slapping strike.

Heel Kick - Soku Yaku Ken - Using the bottom of the foot (ball of foot or heel) to shove into target.

Knee Strike - Sokki Ken - Using the bones of the knee to strike close targets.

Ball Of Foot Kick - Soku Gyaku Ken - Using the tips of toes to strike or jab target.

Body Fist - Tai Ken - Using the hips, shoulders, etc to strike or apply pressure.

Natural Weapons - Shizen Ken - Using teeth, nails or anything else to attack the target.

Kogeki Kata - Attacking Forms
Striking Combinations

Beginner

1. High Block, Punch, Front Stamp Kick
2. Punch, Punch, Right Roundhouse
3. Left Punch, Right Punch, Left Roundhouse, Right Reversed Roundhouse.
4. Right Roundhouse, Left Reversed Roundhouse, Right 360 Crescent Kick.
5. Left Punch, Right Punch, Right Side Stamp Kick, Left Side Stamp Kick
6. Punch, Punch, Elbow, Palm Strike
7. Low Block, Punch, Punch, Forward Stamp Kick.
8. Punch, Punch, Forward Stamp Kick, Reversed Roundhouse.
9. Block And Strike The Attacking Arm, Elbow, Forward Stamp Kick.
10. Punch, Punch, Elbow, Roundhouse

Intermediate

11. Punch, Punch, Roundhouse, Reversed Roundhouse, 360 Crescent Kick.
12. Left High Block, Right High Block, Left Low Block, Right Punch, Reversed Roundhouse.
13. Right Punch, Left Punch, Right Front Stamp Kick, Left

Front Stamp Kick.

14. High Block, Punch, Reversed Roundhouse.

15. Left Punch, Right Elbow Strike, Right Punch, Left Elbow Strike.

16. Left High Block, Right Roundhouse, Right Low Block, Front Stamp Kick.

17. High Block, Palm Heel Strike, Palm Heel Strike, Front Stamp Kick.

18. High Block, Grab, Knee Strike, Knee Strike, Front Stamp Kick.

19. Right High Block, Right Low Block, Left Front Stamp Kick, Left High Block, Left Low Block, Right Front Stamp Kick.

20. Left High Block, Right High Block, Left Punch, Right Punch, Right Elbow Strike, Left Front Stamp Kick.

Advanced

21. Left Punch, Left Punch, Right Punch, Right Back Fist.

22. Left Front Stamp Kick, Right Roundhouse, Right Reversed Roundhouse, Right Reversed Sweep.

23. Right Front Stamp Kick, Right Roundhouse, Left Front Stamp Kick, Left Roundhouse.

24. Right Front Stamp Kick, Right Roundhouse, Left Front Stamp Kick, Right Reversed Roundhouse.

25. Left Punch, Right Punch, Right Elbow Strike, Left Palm Heel Strike, Right Front Stamp Kick.

26. High Block, Left Punch, Right Inside Blade Hande, Left

Front Stamp Kick.

27. Left Low Block, Right High Block, Left Elbow, Front Stamp Kick.

28. Left High Block, Right Palm Heel Strike, Left Punch, Right Roundhouse, Left Front Stamp Kick.

29. Left Crushing Block, Right Crushing Block, Right Front Stamp Kick, Left Front Stamp Kick.

30. Right Outside High Block, Right Punch To Ribs, Left Outside High Block, Left Punch To Ribs.

31. Left Crushing Block, Left Punch, Right Crushing Block, Right Punch.

32. Right Front Stamp Kick, Right Reversed Roundhouse, Left Roundhouse, Right Reversed Roundhouse.

Red Belt - 9th Kyu

Bows correctly

Ties belt correctly

Follows stretching accurately (Junan Taiso)

Falling Forms - Ukemi Gata

Two Handed Forward Roll - Ryote Zenpo Kaiten

Backwards Roll - Koho Kaiten

Backwards Break Fall - Ushiro Ukemi

Sideways Break Fall - Yoko Ukemi

Stances - Kamae

Kneeling Posture - Seiza No Kamae

Natural Standing Posture - Shizen No Kamae

One Line/ Number One Posture - Ichimonji No Kamae

Ichimonji With Rear Hand at Waist Level - Seigan No Kamae

Elemental Forms - Sanshin No Kata

Earth Form - Swinging Strike - Chi No Kata

Strike & Block - Tsuki & Uke

High, Medium and Low Strikes - Jodan, Chudan, Gedan Tsuki.

High, Medium and Low Blocks - Jodan, Chudan, Gedan Uke.

How To Bow Correctly

Opening Ceremony - Shizen Rei (Koto Dama)

At the beginning of the class, all the students shall sit in Seiza No Kamae in a line facing towards the Shidoshi/Sensei (Instructor) and the Kamidana (Dojo Shrine) and place their hands together for the Koto Dama (Spiritual Prayer). The Shidoshi then begins by saying:

"Chihayafuru kami no oseiwa tokosheini tadashiki kokkoro mio mamoruran. Shikin haramitsu dai komyo."

The students then repeat the words "Shikin haramitsu dai komyo" followed by two claps, a bow, then one clap and another bow.

Just before the start of the lesson the Shidoshi says "Onegai shi mas" and bows to the students from Seiza No Kamae. Students then say "Onegai shi mas" and bow back to the Shidoshi. The lesson then starts.

Closing Ceremony - Sensei Ni Rei

At the end of the class, all of the students shall sit in Seiza No Kamae in a line facing towards the Shidoshi/Shihan (Instructor) and the Kamidana (Dojo Shrine).

The highest ranking student in the dojo says the words "Sensei Ni Rei" and the students and Shidoshi bow to one another and say "Arigato Gozeimashta" (Thank You).

Note: Any questions about the day's class or upcoming events are addressed at this point. The lesson then ends.

How To Tie Your Belt Correctly

1. Take your belt and hold a bit about as long as your forearm on your left hip
2. Hold the left hand section of the belt in place and bring the long part of the belt across the front of your body.
3. Make sure it lays flat across your stomach, No twists or folds.
4. Wrap the belt around your back and over the top of the belt on your left hip, still keeping hold of the section sticking out on your left hip. Don't cover in completely.
5. Make sure the belt overlaps and looks like solid bar going all the way around your body.
6. Pull the longer end of the belt underneath the main belt at the front of the body. Underneath from the bottom of the belt not the top.
7. The left hand section and right hand ends of the belt are now pulled to be at equal lengths at the front of the body.
8. The left hand end then goes over the right hand end and ties into a knot.

There are various ways of tying your Obi (Belt) in different martial arts styles but we mainly tie ours this way so that the Saya (sheath of a sword) doesn't get trapped within the folds of the belt when it needed to be used by the Ninja or Samurai.

Its common for the belt to be folded in half and then the middle of the belt to be placed on the belly button and brought around the back, crossed over and tied off. It's very common in Karate, Judo and Tae Kwon Do but we tie our Obi differently when training in Ninjutsu.

Ukemi Gata - Falling Forms

Two Handed Forward Roll - Ryote Zenpo Kaiten

Starting from Shizen No Kamae, place the palms of each hand flat on the floor just in front of you with the fingers of each hand pointing towards each other. Tuck the head in and using the arms to support the body weight, allow the body to roll over naturally using your right foot to push the body over. Finish the roll by landing back on your feet in a position that allows you to stand up naturally.

Backwards Roll - Koho Kaiten

Start from Shizen No Kamae, Drop to a sitting position with the right leg outstretched and forming an arch in your back, roll backwards being sure to keep your head tucked in and your arms forward so as to not catch the elbows on the ground during the roll. Kick the right leg over the left shoulder in an arching fashion and roll over at a 45 degree angle. Return to your feet upon completion of the roll in a smooth natural manner and assume a defensive posture.

Backwards Break Fall - Ushiro Ukemi

Start in Shizen No Kamae, Step back with the left foot and collapse the left leg lowering the body into a seated position with the right leg extended out to the front of the body. Roll backwards onto your back with the momentum of dropping back onto your seat ensuring you keep your head and shoulders off of the floor at all times. Once the roll gets to the middle of the back, slap at 45 degrees either side of the body at waist height.

Note: The force of the Ukemi when you slap can be used to propel the body over into a backwards roll (Koho Kaiten).

Sideways Break Fall - Yoko Ukemi

Start standing or kneeling, Kick the right leg across the left leg and drop down to a position rolling along the right hand side of the body, from the foot to the thigh to the hip, up to the elbow and shoulder ensuring that the head and neck are off of the floor at all times. As the break fall reaches the elbow the right hand slaps the floor to disperse the momentum of the fall.

Stances - Kamae

Kneeling Posture - Seiza No Kamae

Natural Standing Posture - Shizen No Kamae

One Line/ Number One Posture - Ichimonji No Kamae

Ichimonji With Rear Hand at Waist Level - Soshin No Kamae

3 Spirit Forms - Sanshin No Kata

Earth Form - Chi No Kata
3 finger strike (San Shi Tan Ken) to pressure point in the neck. The student starts in Shizen No Kamae, then assumes Soshin No Kamae stepping straight back. The students rear hand drops down and swings straight back to an approximate 45 degree angle to the body. The student steps through with the rear leg and swings the arm up in a manner similar to a pendulum striking with a 3 finger strike (San Shi Tan Ken) to the carotid artery in the neck. This can then be followed up by stepping through and striking with a secondary San Shi Tan Ken with the left hand. It is important to focus on body posture, footwork and big movements.

Strikes & Blocks - Tsuki & Uke

It's important to learn how to perform a basic attack and how to defend against one. This is done by practising your punches on the punchbags/pads and by learning to block an incoming punch thrown by a partner. Start slow and then play with different punching combinations and techniques such as:

- Jab – Quick straight punch
- Cross – Punching across the body
- Hook – Curved punch
- Uppercut – Punching upwards
- Hammerfist – Striking with the bottom of the fist
- Palm Strike – Using the open hand to strike

Some basic punching combinations are:

- Left Jab. Left Jab, Right Cross
- Left Jab, Right Cross, Left Jab, Right Uppercut
- Left Jab, Left Jab, Right Cross, Left Palm, Right Cross
- Right Cross, Left Uppercut, Right Cross, Two Left Jabs.
- Left Jab, Left Jab, Three Right Hammerfists

High, Medium and Low Strikes - Jodan, Chudan, Gedan Tsuki.

Practice punching at high, medium and low levels. Start by stepping through with straight punches and then work on combinations striking at different levels.

High, Medium and Low Blocks - Jodan, Chudan, Gedan Uke

Practice blocking in a circular motion with the leading arm at high, medium and low levels. You can also move to the inside and outside of the incoming punch.

<u>Yellow Belt</u> - 8th Kyu

Stretching - Junan Taiso

Body Massage - Keiko Mae Zen Shin

Deep Breathing - Shin Kokyu Sanadan/ Kokyuho

Dragon Body Stretching - Ryu Tai Endo / Junan Undo

Stretching The Feet And Ankle - Ashi Yubi / Ashi Kubi No Undo

Stretching the Hips - Ashi Soko Awase Zenkutsu

Stretching Both Legs (Apart) - Ashi Hiroge Zenkutsu

Stretching Both Legs (Together) - Ashi Narabe Zenkutsu

Cat Stretching - Sesuji Nobashi

Quadriceps Stretching - Kokjutsu

Stretching the Hands, Shoulders and Neck - Sushi Kata Mawashi

Stretching The Achilles Tendon And Hip Rotations - Heza Koshi No Kusshin

Alternating Shoulder Rolls - Teashi No Furi Mawashi

Falling Forms - Ukemi Gata

Two Handed Forward Roll - Ryote Zenpo Kaiten

Backwards Roll - Koho Kaiten

Backwards Break Fall - Ushiro Ukemi

Sideways Break Fall - Yoko Ukemi

One Handed Forward Roll - Katate Zenpo Kaiten

Sideways Roll - Sokuho Kaiten

Front Break Fall From Kneeling - Mae Ukemi / Zenpo Ukemi

Stances - Kamae

Kneeling Posture - Seiza No Kamae

Natural Standing Posture - Shizen No Kamae

One Line/ Number One Posture - Ichimonji No Kamae

Ichimonji With Rear Hand at Waist Level - Soshin No Kamae

Crossed Arms Posture - Jumonji No Kamae

Number One Posture on One Leg - Hicho No Kamae

Kicks - Keri

Forward Stamp Kick - Zenpo Geri

Sideways Stamp Kick – Sokuho Geri

Elemental Forms - San Shin No Kata – *3 Spirit Forms*

Earth Form - Chi No Kata

Water Form - Sui No Kata

Shi Ho Tenchi Tobi - Four Ways of Leaping

Te Hodoki - Wrist Escapes - *Single handed escapes*

Figure 4 Armlock - Elbow Lock

<u>Junan Taiso</u> - Body Conditioning

The students are not expected to remember all the Japanese terms for gradings as long as they know how to stretch and warm up. There are several important points in Junan Taiso to remember. Listen to and work in harmony with your body for the best results.

Body Massage - Keiko Mae Zen Shin
In a sitting position, starting with the feet, begin to massage the muscles and tendons is the sole of the feet, then the calf muscles, up to the quadriceps , the stomach muscles, then the pectoral muscles, and down either arm to the hands. Be sure to really work out any tension in each muscle group to relax them.

Deep Breathing (Three Methods) - Kokyuho

Frontal Breathing - Shomen Kokyuho
Assume a kneeling (Seiza No Kamae) Position.
Pull back both shoulders opening the shoulders and chest, inhale.
As you drop both shoulders forwards and round the back, exhale completely. Perform this eight time slowly.

Left And Right Deep Breathing - Seiza Sayu Shinkokyu
Assume a kneeling (Seiza No Kamae) position.
Turning to face the right, pulling back the right shoulder, Inhale.
Dropping the right shoulder, turning back to the front, exhale completely.
Likewise inhale turning to the left then exhale completely returning to face forwards. Perform this eight times slowly.

Extension Deep Breathing - Shinten Shikokyu
From a position sitting on the ground, stretch out the hands
and feet directly to the front of the body.
From this four limb extended seat, spread the hands and arms
widely and breathe in deeply.
Close the arms and hands as if to put them forward on top of
the legs, exhale completely. Perform this eight times slowly.

Dragon Body Stretching - Ryu Tai Endo - Junan Undo

Stretching the Feet and Ankles - Ashi Yubi, Ashi Kubi No Undo
Hold the ankle with one hand and the foot with the other and
manually turn the ankle 10 times both clockwise and anti-
clockwise. Lastly, hold the foot by the toes and bend them
backwards and forwards 4 to 5 times.

Stretching the Hips - Ashi Soko Awase Zenkutsu
Sit up straight with the soles of the feet together in your hands,
placing the knees on the floor with the muscles pushing down
(the elbows may be used to assist with the downward pushing
motion if necessary). Repeat this action 8 to 10 times

Stretching Both Legs (Apart) - Ashi Hiroge Zenkutsu
Sit with the back straight, legs directly ahead and open the
legs as far as possible, curl the toes back and lower the trunk
of the body to the floor without bending the knees or upper
back. Repeat this action 8 to 10 times.

Stretching Both Legs (Together) - Ashi Narabe Zenkutsu
Sit with back straight, legs together, directly ahead of you.
Stretching from the lower back, bend forward touching your
knees with your chest and hold your feet. Do not bend your
knees. Repeat this 8 to 10 times.

31

Cat Stretching - Sesuji Nobashi
Lay face down with a straight body, engage the lower back, arching your body upwards, lifting your feet and shoulders off of the floor then place your hands on the floor. Take a deep breath and push up to increase the arc in your back, then exhale and lower back to the floor. Repeat this 4 to 5 times.

Quadriceps Stretching - Kokjutsu
Sit in Seiza No Kamae but with feet slightly apart, sitting directly on the floor. Then lay back slowly, face up with both arms behind your head, and relax into this position. Repeat this carefully, 4 to 5 times.

Stretching Hands, Shoulders and Neck - Sushi Kata Mawashi
Sit in Seiza No Kamae and do the following:

- Manually turn the fingers in circles one by one, clockwise and anti-clockwise, pulling them once or twice
- Clasp your hand together in a large fist and turn them in a figure-of-eight motion, clockwise and anti-clockwise.
- Roll the shoulders backwards and forwards 20 times each direction.
- Slowly rock the head backwards and forwards, ear to shoulder, left to right and roll it clockwise and anti-clockwise, never completing more than a full circle. For each of these, repeat 4 or 5 times.

Stretching Tendons & Hip Rotations - Heza Koshi No Kusshin
While standing, keep the legs straight, bending forwards to stretch the Achilles tendon, repeat this 10 times. Stand with feet apart and bend the knees, place hands on hips and rotate them in a circle clockwise and anti-clockwise, repeat 20 times.

Alternating Shoulder Rolls - Teashi No Furi Mawashi
Roll the arms forwards and backwards so that the hands touch above the head, repeat 20 times.

Falling Forms - Ukemi Gata

Two Handed Forward Roll - Ryote Zenpo Kaiten

Starting from Shizen No Kamae, place the palms of each hand flat on the floor just in front of you with the fingers of each hand pointing towards each other. Tuck the head in and using the arms to support the body weight, allow the body to roll over naturally using your right foot to push the body over. Finish the roll by landing back on your feet in a position that allows you to stand up naturally.

Backwards Roll - Koho Kaiten

Start from Shizen No Kamae, Drop to a sitting position with the right leg outstretched and forming an arch in your back, roll backwards being sure to keep your head tucked in and your arms forward so as to not catch the elbows on the ground during the roll. Kick the right leg over the left shoulder in an arching fashion and roll over at a 45 degree angle. Return to your feet upon completion of the roll in a smooth natural manner and assume a defensive posture.

Backwards Break Fall - Ushiro Ukemi

Start in Shizen No Kamae, Step back with the left foot and collapse the left leg lowering the body into a seated position with the right leg extended out to the front of the body. Roll backwards onto your back with the momentum of dropping back onto your seat ensuring you keep your head and shoulders off of the floor at all times. Once the roll gets to the middle of the back, slap at 45 degrees either side of the body at waist height.

Note: The force of the Ukemi when you slap can be used to propel the body over into Koho Kaiten.

Sideways Break Fall - Yoko Ukemi

Start standing (Shizen No Kamae) or kneeling (Suwari Gata). Kick the right leg across the left leg and drop down to a position rolling along the right hand side of the body, from the foot to the thigh to the hip, up to the elbow and shoulder ensuring that the head and neck are off of the floor at all times. As the Ukemi reaches the elbow the right hand slaps the floor to disperse the momentum of the fall.

One Handed Forward Roll - Katate Zenpo Kaiten

As in Zenpo Kaiten, start in Shizen No Kamae or Suwari Gata and lean forward placing the palm of the right hand flat on the ground, the fingers should be pointing at the left foot at a 45 degree angle. Tuck the head in and allow the body to roll over naturally kicking the body over with the feet.

The momentum of the roll should be dispersed over the right shoulder, down the back, across the left kidney, hip and then the left hand performs a slap on the ground (Ukemi) finish by returning to a position back on your feet in a defensive posture.

Play with your rolling techniques and try to cover longer and shorter distances and different angles. Use your legs.

Note: The position of the hand when placed on the floor before the roll effects the direction of travel, the sharper the angle of the hand and arm, the sharper the angle of the roll.

Sideways Roll - Sokuho Kaiten

Start in Hira Ichimonji No Kamae, Look straight ahead keeping your opponent in sight at all times during the roll, take a step with the right foot and bend the right knee dropping into a low posture and place the palm of the right hand flat on the ground with the fingers pointing to the left and the elbow of the right arm positioned in front of the right knee but not touching it.

The palm of the left hand is then placed flat on the floor next to the right hand in between the knee and the right arm with fingers on the left hand pointing to the right.
The arms are then used to support the body weight and lower the body to the ground while the legs kick the body over. The momentum of the roll is dispersed over the right shoulder across to the left shoulder with Ukemi being performed by the left hand.

Line of sight must be maintained at all times during the roll! Finish the roll by returning to your feet in one continuous motion and assuming Hira Ichimonji No Kamae.

Note: When comfortable with Sokoho Kaiten try leaping into the roll to cover more distance.

Front Break Fall From Kneeling - Zenpo Ukemi / Mae Ukemi

Forward break-fall with one or both hands from standing or kneeling and with a Geri/Keri (Kick). Performed the same as Zenpo Ukemi but with a strong Koho Geri (Backwards Stamp Kick) to the opponent's abdomen or face.

Note: The Koho Geri can also be used to kick off of the opponent and propel the defender into a Zenpo Kaiten to create space.

35

Stances - Kamae

Kneeling Posture - Seiza No Kamae

Natural Standing Posture - Shizen No Kamae

One Line/ Number One Posture - Ichimonji No Kamae

Number One Posture Rear Hand at Waist - Soshin No Kamae

Crossed Arms - Jumonji No Kamae

One Legged Number One Posture - Hicho No Kamae

Starjump Posture - Hira Ichimonji No Kamae

Kicks - Keri

Forward Stamp Kick - Zenpo Geri

Start in Shizen No Kamae, Tori then assumes Ichimonji No Kamae, Tori raises the knee of the right leg to the shoulder and drives the Heel of the right foot through Ukes chest utilizing your body weight to knock them back. Step through with the kick and assume Kamae. This can also be used when pinned against a wall by creating an opening between Tori and Uke with Tori using the wall to provide stability to devastating effect.

Sideways Stamp Kick - Sokuho Geri
Tori starts in Shizen No Kamae, then assumes Ichimonji No Kamae, Tori lifts the knee of the right leg to the shoulder and turns the knee inwards to drive the Sokuho Geri out to the right. It must be mentioned that Sokuho Geri is not a horizontal side snap kick but similar to Zenpo Geri in the way it's performed with the foot positioned vertically.

3 Spirit Forms - San Shin No Kata

Earth Form - Chi No Kata

3 finger strike (San Shi Tan Ken) to pressure point in the neck. The student starts in Shizen No Kamae, then assumes Soshin No Kamae stepping straight back. The students rear hand drops down and swings straight back to an approximate 45 degree angle to the body. The student steps through with the rear leg and swings the arm up in a manner similar to a pendulum striking with a 3 finger strike (San Shi Tan Ken) to the carotid artery in the neck. This can then be followed up by stepping through and striking with a secondary San Shi Tan Ken with the left hand. It is important to focus on body posture, footwork and big movements.

Water Form - Sui No Kata

The student starts is Soshin No Kamae and performs a high block followed by outside Karate chop (Omote Kiten Ken) to the neck.
The student starts in Shizen No Kamae and then assumes Soshin No Kamae stepping back at 45 degrees and assuming a low posture. A high block (Jodan Uke)i is performed with the forehand whilst simultaneously assuming Dokko No Kamae and stepping through with an outside Karate chop (Omote Kiten Ken) strike to the neck. The key point to remember with Sui No Kata is to utilize the energy generated from the twisting motion of the hips when striking and to concentrate on proper footwork and guarding the head in Dokko No Kamae.
Practice the form until it feels smooth and natural on both sides when striking. Start off slowly and then gradually speed it up and remember "If you can't do it slow, You can't do it fast!".

Four Ways of Leaping - Shi Ho Tenchi Tobi

Leaping in four directions but not bounding up and down and keeping level (as with Tsuki). The key is to time the landing of the leap just right so that the rear foot carries you the furthest possible distance. This will be explained more in lesson.

Leaping Forwards - Zenpo Tobi
Leaping Backwards - Koho Tobi
Leaping Right - Migi Tobi
Leaping Left - Hidari Tobi
High And Low Leaping - Hicho Tobi

Wrist Escapes - Te Hodoki - *Gateway Principles*
Using circular motions and angling to escape wrist grabs.

Clockwise Wrist Escape - Omote Te Hodoki
Anticlockwise Wrist Escape - Ura Te Hodoki
Two Handed Grab Escape - Omote Kiten Ken Te Hodoki
Turning Wrist Escape - Uchi Mawashi Te Hodoki

Figure 4 Armlock
The figure 4 armlock is a simple elbow lock. The student starts with the opponent grabbing their left shoulder with the right hand. The student responds by bringing the left arm up and over the opponents right arm bringing it down to the side of the body holding onto it tightly. The student then places their right hand on the opponents left shoulder and brings their left hand under the opponents arm grabbing the right arm at the elbow (Making an upside down 4 shape with the students arms). The student then pushes down with the right hand and uses the fingers of the left hand to apply pressure to the locked elbow.

Orange belt - 7th kyu

Stretching - Junan Taiso

Body Massage - Keiko Mae Zen Shin

Deep Breathing - Shin Kokyu Sanadan/ Kokyuho

Dragon Body Stretching - Ryu Tai Endo / Junan Undo

Stretching The Feet And Ankles - Ashi Yubi / Ashi Kubi No Undo

Stretching the Hips - Ashi Soko Awase Zenkutsu

Stretching Both Legs (Apart) - Ashi Hiroge Zenkutsu

Stretching Both Legs (Together) - Ashi Narabe Zenkutsu

Cat Stretching - Sesuji Nobashi

Quadriceps Stretching - Kokjutsu

Stretching the Hands, Shoulders and Neck - Sushi Kata Mawashi

Stretching The Achilles Tendon And Hip Rotations - Heza Koshi No Kusshin

Alternating Shoulder Rolls - Teashi No Furi Mawashi

Falling Forms - Ukemi Gata

Two Handed Forward Roll - Ryote Zenpo Kaiten

Backwards Roll - Koho Kaiten

Backwards Break Fall - Ushiro Ukemi

Sideways Break Fall - Yoko Ukemi

One Handed Forward Roll - Katate Zenpo Kaiten

Sideways Roll - Sokuho Kaiten

Front Break Fall With Back Kick - Mae Ukemi

No Handed Forward Roll - Mute Zenpo Kaiten

Sideways Flow - Yoko Nagare

Stances - Kamae

Kneeling Posture - Seiza No Kamae

Natural Standing Posture - Shizen No Kamae

One Line/ Number One Posture - Ichimonji No Kamae

One Line With Rear Hand at Waist Level - Soshin No Kamae

Crossed Arms - Jumonji No Kamae

One Legged Ichimonji No Kamae - Hicho No Kamae

One Line With Rear Arm Protecting Face - Dokko No Kamae

Covering Opponents Eyes - Kosei No Kamae

Kicks - Keri

Forward Stamp Kick - Zenpo Geri

Sideways Stamp Kick - Sokuho Geri

Backwards Stamp Kick - Koho Geri

Heel Kick - Sokuyaku Ken

Ball Of Foot Kick - Sokugyaku Ken

Top Of Foot Kick - Keri Gaeshi

Elemental Forms - San Shin No Kata - *3 Spirit Forms*

Earth Form - Chi No Kata
Water Form - Sui No Kata
Fire Form - Ka No Kata

4 Ways Of Leaping - Shi Ho Tenchi Tobi

Leaping Forwards - Zenpo Tobi
Leaping Backwards - Koho Tobi
Leaping Right - Migi Tobi
Leaping Left - Hidari Tobi

High And Low Leaping - Hicho Tobi

Wrist Escapes - Te Hodoki

Single Handed Escapes - Katate Te Hodoki

Double Handed Escapes - Ryote Te Hodoki

Ninja Balancing Walk - Shinobi Aruki

Basic Striking Forms - Beginner Level of the Kogeki Kata

Falling Forms - Ukemi Gata

Two Handed Forward Roll - Ryote Zenpo Kaiten

Starting from standing or kneeling, place the palms of each hand flat on the floor just in front of you with the fingers of each hand pointing towards each other. Tuck the head in and using the arms to support the body weight, allow the body to roll over naturally using your right foot to push the body over. Finish the roll by landing back on your feet in a position that allows you to stand up naturally.

Backwards Roll - Koho Kaiten

Start from standing, Drop to a sitting position with the right leg outstretched and forming an arch in your back, roll backwards being sure to keep your head tucked in and your arms forward so as to not catch the elbows on the ground during the roll. Kick the right leg over the left shoulder in an arching fashion and roll over at a 45 degree angle. Return to your feet upon completion of the roll in a smooth natural manner and assume a defensive posture (Ichimonji No Kamae).

Backwards Break Fall - Ushiro Ukemi

Start standing (Shizen No Kamae), Step back with the left foot and collapse the left leg lowering the body into a seated position with the right leg extended out to the front of the body. Roll backwards onto your back with the momentum of dropping back onto your seat ensuring you keep your head and shoulders off of the floor at all times. Once the roll gets to the middle of the back, slap at 45 degrees either side of the body at waist height.
Note: The force of the Ukemi when you slap can be used to propel the body over into a Backwards Roll (Koho Kaiten).

42

Sideways Break Fall - Yoko Ukemi

Start standing (Shizen No Kamae) or kneeling (Suwari Gata). Kick the right leg across the left leg and drop down to a position rolling along the right hand side of the body, from the foot to the thigh to the hip, up to the elbow and shoulder ensuring that the head and neck are off of the floor at all times.

As the Ukemi reaches the elbow the right hand slaps the floor to disperse the momentum of the fall.

One Handed Forward Roll - Katate Zenpo Kaiten

Start in standing (Shizen No Kamae) or kneeling (Suwari Gata) and lean forward placing the palm of the right hand flat on the ground, the fingers should be pointing at the left foot at a 45 degree angle. Tuck the head in and allow the body to roll over naturally kicking the body over with the feet.

The momentum of the roll should be dispersed over the right shoulder, down the back, across the left kidney and hip, the left hand performs a slap and finish by returning to a position back on your feet in a defensive posture (Ichimonji No Kamae).

Note: The position of the hand when placed on the floor before the roll effects the direction of travel, the sharper the angle of the hand and arm, the sharper the angle of the roll.

Sideways Roll - Sokuho Kaiten

Start in a Starjump Posture (Hira Ichimonji No Kamae). Look straight ahead keeping your opponent in sight at all times during the roll, take a step with the right foot and bend the right knee dropping into a low posture and place the palm of the right hand flat on the ground with the fingers pointing to the left and the elbow of the right arm positioned in front of the right knee but not touching it. The palm of the left hand is then placed flat on the floor next to the right hand in between the knee and the right arm with fingers on the left hand pointing to the right.

The arms are then used to support the body weight and lower the body to the ground while the legs kick the body over. The momentum of the roll is dispersed over the right shoulder across to the left shoulder with Ukemi being performed by the left hand.

Line of sight must be maintained at all times during the roll! Finish the roll by returning to your feet in one continuous motion and assuming Hira Ichimonji No Kamae.

Note: When comfortable with Soko Ho Kaiten try leaping into the roll to cover more distance.

Front Break Fall From Kneeling - Mae Ukemi
Forward break-fall with one or both hands from standing or kneeling and with a Geri/Keri (Kick). Performed the same as Zenpo Ukemi but with a strong Koho Geri (Backwards Stamp Kick) to the opponent's abdomen or face.

No Handed Forward Roll - Mute Zenpo Kaiten
Start in Shizen No Kamae, Step Forward with the right foot, tuck the head in and engaging the right arm and shoulder generate enough momentum to throw the body over kicking off with the feet so that the head is clear of the ground and the roll is performed by rolling onto the right shoulder in one simultaneous motion. Roll is finished by returning to the feet and standing up in a defensive posture.

Sideways Flow - Yoko Nagare
Start in a standing position (Shizen No Kamae), Then assume
a Starjump Posture (Hira Ichimonji No Kamae),
Swing the right leg across the front of the left leg placing the
outer edge of the right foot on the ground first. Lower the body
down with the left leg so that you are now sat on the floor with
the right leg extending to the left and allow the momentum of
the movement to roll the body over into Koho Kaiten.
It is important to mention that Yoko Nagare must be done in
one fluid motion or the momentum behind the movement is not
enough to kick the body over effectively. As the right leg
moves across in front of the left from Hira Ichimonji No Kamae
both of the arms swing down and cross in front of the body.
This is done to avoid the temptation to place the hand flat on
the floor breaking the wrist.

<u>Stances</u> - Kamae

Kneeling Posture - Seiza No Kamae

Sitting With One Leg Ready to Stand - Fudoza No Kamae

Natural Standing Posture - Shizen No Kamae

One Line/ Number One Posture - Ichimonji No Kamae

Ichimonji With Rear Hand at Waist Level - Soshin No Kamae

Crossed Arms - Jumonji No Kamae

One Legged Ichimonji No Kamae - Hicho No Kamae

One Line With Rear Arm Protecting Face - Dokko No Kamae

Covering Opponents Eyes - Kosei No Kamae

<u>Kicks</u> - Keri

Forward Stamp Kick - Zenpo Geri
Start standing, Then assume the One Line Posture. Raise the
knee of the right leg to the shoulder and drives the Heel of the
right foot through the opponents chest utilizing your body
weight to knock them back. Step through with the kick and
assume Kamae. This can also be used when pinned against a
wall by creating an opening between the defender (Tori) and
the attacker (Uke) with defender using the wall to provide
stability..

Sideways Stamp Kick - Sokuho Geri
Start standing, then assumes the One Line Posture. Raise the
knee of the right leg to the shoulder and turn the knee inwards
to drive the Sideways Stamp Kick (Sokuho Geri) out to the
right. It must be mentioned that Sideways Stamp Kick is not a
horizontal Side Snap Kick but similar to a Forward Stamp Kick
in the way it's performed with the foot positioned vertically.

Backwards Stamp Kick - Koho Geri
Start standing, Then assume a Crossed Arms Posture
(Jumonji No Kamae). The student lifts the knee of the right leg
to the chest and then drives the right foot back into the
opponents Groin/Stomach swinging the arms down with the
kick to generate momentum. A Backwards Stamp Kick can
also be used to kick off of the opponent and perform a
Forwards Roll.

Heel Kick - Sokuyaku Ken
Using the heel of the foot to kick the opponent. This could be in
a similar way to your Front Stamp Kick or using the back of
your heel like a hammer when doing an Axe Kick. Any kick
where you strike with the heel is considered a Sokuyaku Ken.

46

Ball Of Foot Kick - Sokugyaku Ken
Using the ball of the foot to kick the opponent. This could be in a similar way to your Front Stamp Kick or using the ball of the foot to strike like when performing a Reverse Roundhouse. Any kick where you dig in, push or strike with the ball of the foot is considered a Sokugyaku Ken.

Top Of Foot Kick - Keri Gaeshi
Using the top of the foot to kick the opponent. This is kicking in a natural way like kicking a football swinging the leg. A good example of the top of the foot kick is kicking to the groin (Suzu) or even a roundhouse as your kicking with the top of the foot

3 Spirit Forms - San Shin No Kata

Earth Form - Chi No Kata
3 finger strike (San Shi Tan Ken) to pressure point in the neck. The student starts in Shizen No Kamae, then assumes Soshin No Kamae stepping straight back. The students rear hand drops down and swings straight back to an approximate 45 degree angle to the body. The student steps through with the rear leg and swings the arm up in a manner similar to a pendulum striking with a 3 finger strike (San Shi Tan Ken) to the carotid artery in the neck. This can then be followed up by stepping through and striking with a secondary San Shi Tan Ken with the left hand. It is important to focus on body posture, footwork and big movements.

Water Form - Sui No Kata
The student starts is Soshin No Kamae and performs a high block followed by outside Karate chop (Omote Kiten Ken) to the neck.
The student starts in Shizen No Kamae and then assumes Soshin No Kamae stepping back at 45 degrees and assuming

47

a low posture. A high block (Jodan Uke)i is performed with the forehand whilst simultaneously assuming Dokko No Kamae and stepping through with an outside Karate chop (Omote Kiten Ken) strike to the neck. The key point to remember with Sui No Kata is to utilize the energy generated from the twisting motion of the hips when striking and to concentrate on proper footwork and guarding the head in Dokko No Kamae.

Practice the form until it feels smooth and natural on both sides when striking. Start off slowly and then gradually speed it up and remember "If you can't do it slow, You can't do it fast!"

Fire Form - Ka No Kata
The student starts in Shizen No Kamae and then assumes Soshin No Kamae stepping back at 45 degrees and assuming a low defensive posture. Tori performs a High Block (Jodan Uke), assumes Dokko No Kamae and steps through with an Inside Karate Chop (Kiten Ken) strike to the opponents neck. The key point to remember is to utilize Taijutsu and drop the bodyweight down when the strike makes contact with the Ukes neck.

Four Ways of Leaping - Shi Ho Tenchi Tobi
Leaping in four directions but not bounding up and down and keeping level (as with Tsuki). The key is to time the landing of the leap just right so that the rear foot carries you the furthest possible distance. This will be explained more in lesson.

Leaping Forwards - Zenpo Tobi
Leaping Backwards - Koho Tobi
Leaping Right - Migi Tobi
Leaping Left - Hidari Tobi
High And Low Leaping - Hicho Tobi

Wrist Escapes - Te Hodoki

Single Handed Escapes - Katate Te Hodoki

Single Hand Release - Uchi Mawashi
Uchi Mawashi is performed by using superior angling and proper technique to break the opponents grip. The student starts in Shizen No Kamae, The opponent reaches in and grabs Tori's right wrist with the left hand.

The student responds by lifting the right arm up in a large anti-clockwise circle whilst stepping forwards at a 45 degree angle off to the side of Uke. The student then steps back with the left foot pivoting at 90 degrees and gets his elbow as close to the opponents elbow as possible.

The student strikes his hand downwards still travelling in an anticlockwise manner. Ukes hand is automatically released due to the angle of Ukes arm and the centripetal force generated by the anticlockwise motion of the students arm.

The opponent should be left open to a follow up attack due to his inability to reposition himself in time.

This is done in the same direction of the held hand at all times whether the technique is performed on the right (Migi) or left (Hidari).

Note: There are a variety of Henka for Uchi Mawashi that mostly end with a lock being applied once the technique has been performed by the Tori.

Double Handed Escapes - Ryote Te Hodoki

Inner Wrist Twist Double Handed Escape - Ura Gyaku Ryote Te Hodoki
The student starts in Shizen No Kamae, the opponent reaches across and grabs both of the students wrists so that's the arms are parallel.

The student responds by stepping back with the left leg and bending the elbow of the left arm outwards so that the palm is facing downwards and the left arm is horizontally in alignment with the opponents right arm.

The student then steps back in with the left foot and pulls the hand of the left arm in towards their body releasing the left wrist from Ukes grip.

The students left hand then pins the opponents left hand palm down at the wrist securing it in position.

The student encircles the right wrist anticlockwise forming a bend in the opponents wrist, laying the palm of the right hand on top of the opponents wrist and grabbing it on the inside.

The student grabs the hand that was previously pinned in position and steps forward at 45 degrees with the right foot drawing the opponents arm across the students body.

The student then repositions the right arm and using the edge of the forearm applies pressure to the back of the opponents arm on the elbow/tricep muscle and steps back with the left foot at 90 degrees utilizing a twisting motion in the upper body to bring the opponent face first down on the ground.

Ninja Walk - Shinobi Aruki

Shinobi Aruki is important. The overall aim of Shinobi Aruki is to hide the shape of the body when moving through an open area to avoid a silhouette being distinguished by any onlookers.

Start in Shizen No Kamae, then assume Hira Ichimonji No Kamae and bend the knees to drop the body weight and find your centre of gravity. Now lower the arms so that they are outstretched at a 45 degree angle either side of the body.

In this example I am outlining Shinobi Aruki when being

performed to the right but it is the same for the left just the opposite feet.

Whilst in your low Hira Ichimonji No Kamae, Step behind the right leg with the left leg about shoulder width apart and place the toes of the left foot down first, then the ball and heel, bending the knees of both legs so that you are in a low balanced posture.

The arms swing down and cross at the wrists at waist level as the step is taken. The body weight is then transferred to the left leg and the hips move across in a steady level manner, the right leg steps across at about shoulder width apart, the arms swing up so as to assume Hira Ichimonji No Kamae once again and the technique is repeated for the next step.

Basic Attacking Forms - Beginner Level of the Kogeki Kata

At this point in your training you should be practising at home and looking at how to apply the techniques you have learned so far in a realistic way which means learning to attack. For your Orange Belt grading we want to see 3 practised combos demonstrated on the bags, a list of some potential attacking combinations we call the Kogeki Kata (Attacking Forms) can be found on page 19. I have listed 3 simple combinations for you to practice below:

- **Left Punch, Right Punch, Right Roundhouse**

- **Left Punch, Right Punch, Left Roundhouse, Right Reversed Roundhouse**

- **Low Block, Punch, Punch, Forward Stamp Kick**

<u>Orange Belt With Black Stripe</u> – 6th Kyu

Stretching - Junan Taiso

As per previous grades.

Falling Forms - Ukemi Gata

Two Handed Forward Roll - Ryote Zenpo Kaiten

Backwards Roll - Koho Kaiten

Backwards Break Fall - Ushiro Ukemi

Sideways Break Fall - Yoko Ukemi

One Handed Forward Roll - Katate Zenpo Kaiten

Sideways Roll - Sokuho Kaiten

Front Break Fall With Back Kick (Koho Geri) - Mae Ukemi

No Handed Forward Roll - Mute Zenpo Kaiten

Sideways Flow - Yoko Nagare

As per previous grades plus

Stances - Kamae

Kneeling Posture - Seiza No Kamae

Sitting On One Leg Ready to Stand - Fudoza No Kamae

Natural Standing Posture - Shizen No Kamae

One Line/ Number One Posture - Ichimonji No Kamae

One Line With Rear Hand at Waist Level - Soshin No Kamae

Crossed Arms - Jumonji No Kamae

One Legged Number One Posture - Hicho No Kamae

One Line With Rear Arm Protecting Face - Dokko No Kamae

Covering Opponents Eyes - Kosei No Kamae

Kneeling Posture - Suwari Gata

Arms up / Angry Bear Posture - Hokko No Kamae

Arms Spread Wide Stance - Hira Ichimonji No Kamae

Kicks - Keri

Jumping Front Stamp Kick - Katate Tobi Geri

Two Legged Jumping Kick - Ryote Tobi Geri

Roundhouse Kick - Mawashi Geri

Reverse Roundhouse Kick - Gyaku Mawashi Geri

Side Snap Kick - Yoko Geri

Reverse Side Snap Kick - Gyaku Yoko Geri

Flying Side Kick - Yoko Tobi Geri

Hook Kick - Kagi Keri

Axe Kick - Kakato Geri

Elemental Forms - San Shin No Kata - *3 Spirit Forns*

Earth Form - Chi No Kata
Water Form - Sui No Kata
Fire Form - Ka No Kata
Wind Form - Fu no Kata

Fundamental 8 Kata - Kihon Happo No Kata

3 Fundamental Kata - Kihon Koshi Sanpo

Number One Kata - Ichimonji No Kata

Swordsmanship - Kenjutsu - *Bokken*

Wearing a Sword - Taito

Can Name Parts Of The Sword - Koshirae

2 V's - Holding The Sword Correctly

Sitting With One Leg Ready to Stand - Fudoza No Kamae

Sword Pointing At Opponents Eyes - Seigan No Kamae

Sword 45 Degrees Above The Head - Daijodan No Kamae

4 Ways Of Leaping - Shi Ho Tenchi Tobi

Leaping Avoiding Rubber Shuriken

Hicho Tobi - High And Low Jump To Avoid Low Attacks

Te Hodoki - Wrist Escapes

Tai Hodoki - Body Escapes

Rear Body Grab Escape

Shinobi Aruki - Ninja Balancing Walk

Beginner Level of the Kogeki Kata - Basic Striking Forms
Master 3 Basic Combos

Stances - Kamae

Kneeling Posture - Seiza No Kamae

Sitting On One Leg Ready to Stand - Fudoza No Kamae

Natural Standing Posture - Shizen No Kamae

One Line/ Number One Posture - Ichimonji No Kamae

One Line With Rear Hand at Waist Level - Soshin No Kamae

Crossed Arms - Jumonji No Kamae

One Legged Number One Posture - Hicho No Kamae

One Line With Rear Arm Protecting Face - Dokko No Kamae

Covering Opponents Eyes - Kosei No Kamae

Kneeling Posture - Suwari Gata

Arms up / Angry Bear Posture - Hokko No Kamae

Arms Spread Wide Stance - Hira Ichimonji No Kamae

Kicks - Keri

Jumping Front Stamp Kick - Katate Tobi Geri

The student starts in Shizen No Kamae and then brings the hands up to protect their face. The student performs a short fake kick with the left leg and performs a powerful jumping Front Stamp Kick. It's important that the switching of the kicks is quick to draw the opponent into thinking that your kicking with the left leg and then you kick with the right. Also known as the Crane Kick in the Dojo.

Two Legged Jumping Kick - Ryote Tobi Geri

The student starts In Shizen No Kamae, Then takes a slight run up towards the opponent and jumps up lifting both knees to the chest and bringing the hands up above the head in Claws (Shako Ken). The kick is performed by driving the soles of both feet through the opponent and then kicking off of the opponents body to land and perform a backwards roll (Koho Kaiten). To finish the student returns to his feet and assumes Number One Posture (Ichiminji No Kamae).

Roundhouse Kick - Mawashi Geri

A Roundhouse Kick (Mawashi Geri) is a rotating kick to the opponent. This is done by using your arms and body to spin around and opening the hips to propel the kick powerfully towards the opponent with enough momentum to strike with the top of the foot. This will be demonstrated during lessons.

Reverse Roundhouse Kick - Gyaku Mawashi Geri

A Reverse Roudhouse Kick (Gyaku Mawashi Geri) is a backwards rotating high kick to the opponents head. This is done by using your arms and body to spin around, looking and opening the hips to extend the kick high towards the opponent with enough momentum to strike with the sole or heel of the foot. Break it down into 3 parts at first, Assuming Number One Posture, Looking over your shoulder and then turning to perform the kick. This will be demonstrated during lessons.

Note: The Mawashi Geri and Gyaku Mawashi Geri are quite demanding kicks at first. Its good practice to develop the muscles in the legs with static training (Holding each leg out at waist height for 30 secs while standing) and by stretching using Junan Taiiso and partner stretching.

Side Snap Kick - Yoko Geri

The student starts in a standing position (Shizen No Kamae) and then assumes the Number One Posture (Ichimonji No Kamae) with the left foot leading. The student turns to the left raising the right leg into a chambered position turning the left foot so that its pointing to the rear. The student then stamps out to the side with the foot horizontal performing the Side Snap Kick. The kicking leg is then brought back into the chambered position and the student brings the foot back down to the ground assuming the Number One Posture (Ichimonji No Kamae) with the left foot leading. To perform the kick with the left leg lead with the right foot when in your Number One Posture (Ichimonji No Kamae).

Note: You can perform Side Snap Kicks in various ways such as the Step In Side Snap Kick where you do a slight leap to advance towards the opponent and kick with the leading leg.

Reverse Side Snap Kick - Gyaku Yoko Geri

The same as a Side Snap Kick (Yoko Geri) but you spin to the rear and perform the kick. The student starts in a standing position (Shizen No Kamae) and then assumes the Number One Posture (Ichimonji No Kamae) with the left foot leading. The student turns to the right raising the leg into a chambered position as they rotate around. The student then stamps out to the side with the foot horizontal performing the Reverse Side Snap Kick (Gyaku Yoko Geri). The kicking leg is then brought back into the chambered position and the student brings the foot back down to the ground assuming the Number One Posture (Ichimonji No Kamae) with the left foot leading. To perform the kick with the left leg lead with the right foot when in your Number One Posture (Ichimonji No Kamae).

Flying Side Kick - Yoko Tobi Geri

The student starts in a standing position (Shizen No Kamae) and then takes a slight run up towards the opponent. The student jumps and turns sideways leading with a side kick with the right foot and lifting the left leg off of the floor to avoid it being swept out from under them by the opponent. The Flying Side Kick (Yoko Tobi Geri) is performed by driving the sole of the foot through the opponent and then kicking off of the opponents body to land on the left foot and assume the Number One Posture (Ichimonji No Kamae). This is your classic flying kick that you see in movies and video games.

Hook Kick - Kagi Keri

Using the back of the leg to sweep and strike in a hooking motion. This can be done during a throw such as the Outside Hip Throw (Osote Gake) sweeping the opponents legs from under them or alternatively in a manner similar to the Side Snap Kick (Yoko Geri) but kicking just past the opponents face and then hooking back with the leg to strike with the heel or sole of the foot. The Hook Kick can be useful if you want to misdirect the opponent with the first kick.

Axe Kick - Kakato Geri

Slamming the heel down on top of the opponent to strike. The student starts in a standing position (Shizen No Kamae) and then assumes the Number One Posture (Ichimonji No Kamae). The student kicks with the right leg swinging it through in a clockwise arc and once the leg is high slams it straight down striking the opponent with the back of the foot. The Axe Kick is all about generating power by slamming the foot down onto the opponent and is mainly useful if the opponent is one the ground, However it can be used on a standing opponent just be careful not to catch your leg and lose your balance!

3 Spirit Forms - San Shin No Kata

Earth Form - Chi No Kata
3 finger strike (San Shi Tan Ken) to pressure point in the neck. The student starts in Shizen No Kamae, then assumes Soshin No Kamae stepping straight back. The students rear hand drops down and swings straight back to an approximate 45 degree angle to the body. The student steps through with the rear leg and swings the arm up in a manner similar to a pendulum striking with a 3 finger strike (San Shi Tan Ken) to the carotid artery in the neck. This can then be followed up by stepping through and striking with a secondary San Shi Tan Ken with the left hand. It is important to focus on body posture, footwork and big movements.

Water Form - Sui No Kata
The student starts is Soshin No Kamae and performs a high block followed by outside Karate chop (Omote Kiten Ken) to the neck.

The student starts in Shizen No Kamae and then assumes Soshin No Kamae stepping back at 45 degrees and assuming a low posture. A high block (Jodan Uke)i is performed with the forehand whilst simultaneously assuming Dokko No Kamae and stepping through with an outside Karate chop (Omote Kiten Ken) strike to the neck. The key point to remember with Sui No Kata is to utilize the energy generated from the twisting motion of the hips when striking and to concentrate on proper footwork and guarding the head in Dokko No Kamae.

Practice the form until it feels smooth and natural on both sides when striking. Start off slowly and then gradually speed it up and remember "If you can't do it slow, You can't do it fast!"

Fire Form - Ka No Kata
The student starts in Shizen No Kamae and then assumes Soshin No Kamae stepping back at 45 degrees and assuming a low defensive posture. Tori performs a High Block (Jodan Uke), assumes Dokko No Kamae and steps through with an Inside Karate Chop (Kiten Ken) strike to the opponents neck. The key point to remember is to utilize Taijutsu and drop the bodyweight down when the strike makes contact with the Ukes neck.

Wind Form - Fu No Kata
The student starts in a standing position (Shizen No Kamae) and then assumes Soshin No Kamae stepping back at a 45 degree angle with the right foot and dropping into a low posture. The student performs a low block (Gedan Uke) in an circular manner and proceeds to step back in towards opponent with the right foot. The student then steps straight back with the left foot and performs a Thumb Driving Fist (Shito Ken) strike to the ribs/hips utilizing the twisting motion of the hips and effective body movement. The student should move in a semi circular manner when performing the strike really driving it into the opponents ribs (Butsumetsu).

Fundamental 8 Kata - Kihon Happo No Kata
3 Fundamental Kata - Kihon Koshi Sanpo

Number One Kata - Ichimonji No Kata

High Block (Jodan Uke) stepping off at 45 degrees followed by Outside Karate Chop (Omote Kiten Ken) to the opponents neck. Remember the 3 stances Ichimonji No Kamae, Dokko No Kamae and Ichimonji No Kamae when doing the Kata.

60

Swordsmanship - Kenjutsu - *Bokken*

Wearing a Sword - Taito

Taito is the way that we wear and carry a Katana (sword) in the Obi (Belt). There are several important points to mention but a sword is not a toy, even if it is foam or plastic. Real swords should never be handled by a child its far too dangerous, Anything with a real blade should only be handled by an adult with years of training in martial arts.

When you wear or carry a sword you always carry it in the folds of your belt around your waist with the curve of the sword facing upwards. The sword shouldn't be on your side but laying in the front of your belt near your stomach.

Your instructor will demonstrate during lessons but always train safely and only ever train with plastic or foam swords under the supervision of a qualified and insured martial arts instructor.

Name The Parts Of The Sword - Koshirae

Koshirae are the parts or fittings that make a Katana. When you learn the way of the sword you have to learn about them.

- **Handle** - Tsuka

- **Handle Wrap** - Tsuka Ito

- **Handguard** - Tsuba

- **Blade Collar** - Habaki

- **Blade** - Ken

- **Sharp Tip** - Kissaki

2 V's - Holding The Sword Correctly

When using a Katana (Sword) its important to hold it correctly so that you have as much control over the handle as possible. This is done by using a technique we call the 2 V's, When you pick up a sword your right hand should be placed just under the Tsuba (Hand Guard) in a wide pistol grip and your left hand placed around the very end of the handle (Fuchi). It's important that your hands aren't too close together to have leverage over the handle. Line up the 2 V's formed between the thumb and forefingers of each hand along the back of the handle and you will be holding the sword correctly.

Sitting On One Leg Ready to Stand - Fudoza No Kamae

Sword Pointing At Ukes Eyes - Seigan No Kamae

Sword 45 Degrees Above The Head - Daijodan No Kamae

4 Ways Of Leaping - Shi Ho Tenchi Tobi

This time avoiding rubber Shuriken thrown by a partner.

High And Low Jump To Avoid Low Attacks - Hicho Tobi

Avoiding Low Attacks (Ashi Barai) from a Shinai or Bo.

Body Escapes - Tai Hodoki - *Rear Body Grab Escape*

The opponent grabs you from behind pinning your arms. Bend your knees and puff out your shoulders. Backwards Headbutt (Koho Kikaku Ken) to nose, step behind Uke, strike to Suzu and assume Hira Ichimonji No Kamae to trip Uke backwards.

Green Belt – 5th Kyu

To Move In Harmony With Force - Shizen Gyu Ryu Sui

The total body movement is refined for grace and naturalness in all actions. Power becomes a result of mere movement; evasiveness becomes a result of just slight adjustment of body position.

Stretching - Junan Taiso

As in previous grades.

Falling Forms - Ukemi Gata

As in previous grades.

Backwards Roll With Kick - Koho Kaiten Geri

Twisting Flow - Gyaku Nagare

Stances - Kamae

Kneeling Posture - Seiza No Kamae

Natural Standing Posture - Shizen No Kamae

One Line/ Number One Posture - Ichimonji No Kamae

One Line With Rear Hand at Waist Level - Soshin No Kamae

Crossed Arms - Jumonji No Kamae

One Legged Number One Posture - Hicho No Kamae

One Line With Rear Arm Protecting Face - Dokko No Kamae

Covering Opponents Eyes - Kosei No Kamae

Kneeling Posture - Suwari Gata

Arms up / Angry Bear Posture - Hokko No Kamae

Arms Spread Wide Stance - Hira Ichimonji No Kamae

Punching Left And Right - Ihen No Kamae (Migi & Hidari)

Prayer Position - Kongo Gassho No Kamae

Kicks - Keri

Low And High Roundhouse - Gedan and Jodan Mawashi Geri

360 Crescent Kick - San Hyaku Rokku Ju Mawashi Geri

Checking - Sokuyaku Suihei Keri

Sweeping The Leg - Sokuyaku Barai Keri

Knee Strikes - Sokki Ken

4 Ways Of Leaping - Shi Ho Tenchi Tobi

High And Low Jump - Hicho Tobi - To Avoid Incoming Low (Gedan) And High (Jodan) Shinai (Bamboo Sword) Strikes.

Elemental Forms - San Shin No Kata

Earth Form - Chi No Kata
Water Form - Sui No Kata
Fire Form - Ka No Kata
Wind Form - Fu no Kata
Void Form - Ku No Kata

Fundamental 8 Kata - Kihon Happo No Kata

3 Fundamental Kata - Kihon Koshi Sanpo

Number 1 Kata, Straight Step - Ichimonji No Kata
One Legged Kata, Cross Step - Hicho No Kata

Crossed Arms Kata, Zig Zag Step - Jumonji No Kata

Grappling - Jutaijutsu

Defence Against Throws - Nage Kaeshi

False Punch - Okyo

Capture The Head - Zu Dori

Tip By Wind - Fu Kan

Crazy Snow - Ransetsu

Wrist Escapes - Te Hodoki

Body Escapes - Tai Hodoki

Ninja Walk - Shinobi Aruki

Ninja Walk Throwing Shuriken - Shinobi Aruki With Shuriken

Blade Throwing Art - Shurikenjutsu

Senban Shuriken - Into Nets From Standing

Bo Shuriken - Into Paper From Standing

Intermediate Level of the Kogeki Kata – Striking Forms

Falling Forms - Ukemi Gata

Backwards Roll With Kick - Koho Kaiten Geri

This is a Backwards Roll (Koho Kaiten) with the kick performed either before rolling backwards or after to create space (Miai) between the student and the opponent.

Twisting Flow - Gyaku Nagare

Start standing (Shizen No Kamae), Then assume the Number One Posture (Ichimonji No Kamae). Transfer the majority of the body weight to the rear leg and turn the upper body around 180 degrees whilst maintaining the Number One Posture (Ichimonji No Kamae). Bring the right arm down to the ground with the intention of rolling in a direction a further 90 degrees to the left. Kick off with the feet and roll to the left, returning to your feet in one fluid motion ready to flee or assume Kamae.

Stances - Kamae

Kneeling Posture - Seiza No Kamae

Natural Standing Posture - Shizen No Kamae

One Line/ Number One Posture - Ichimonji No Kamae

One Line With Rear Hand at Waist Level - Soshin No Kamae

Crossed Arms - Jumonji No Kamae

One Legged Number One Posture - Hicho No Kamae

One Line With Rear Arm Protecting Face - Dokko No Kamae

Covering Opponents Eyes - Kosei No Kamae

Kneeling Posture - Suwari Gata

Arms up / Angry Bear Posture - Hokko No Kamae

Arms Spread Wide Stance - Hira Ichimonji No Kamae

Punching Left And Right - Ihen No Kamae (Migi & Hidari)

Prayer Position - Kongo Gassho No Kamae

Kicks - Keri

Low And High Roundhouse - Gedan and Jodan Mawashi Geri

Similar to your normal Roundhouse (Mawashi Geri) but this time you kick low and then raise the leg to kick high in the same motion. The student starts in the Number One Posture (Ichimonji No Kamae). The student brings their hands up in front of their face to form a guard and then swings in a low kick with the rear leg opening the hips. Upon completing the first low kick the student raises the same leg and kicks the opponent in the head. These two kicks are done in one continuous motion forming the Low and High Roundhouse (Gedan and Jodan Mawashi Geri)

360 Crescent Kick - San Hyaku Rokku Ju Mawashi Geri

Also know as the Tornado Kick the 360 Crescent Kick involves spinning the body to generate enough force for an extremely powerful kick. Timing is key! You have to set the opponent up to perform the 360 Crescent Kick for example performing a combo and then doing the 360 Crescent Kick while the opponent is stunned. The student starts in the Number One Posture (Ichimonji No Kamae) with the left foot leading. The student then steps through with the right foot moving closer to the opponent. The student continues to turn and raises the left leg. The student then jumps up and kicks over the left leg with a right Roundhouse whilst continuing the turn kicking the opponent in the face. This kick takes a lot of practice and will be demonstrated during the lessons.

Checking – Sokuyaku Suihei Keri

Checking is the action of stopping an opponents kick with the sole of the foot. The student starts in the Number One Posture (Ichimonji No Kamae) and the opponent begins to perform a Natural Kick (Sanshin Keri) swinging the foot. The student sees the incoming kick and steps through with the back foot using the sole of the foot to stop the opponents kick from being fully extended and kicking it back towards the opponent. You often see this in old Kung Fu movies where they stop each other from kicking.

Sweeping The Leg – Sokuyaku Barai Keri

Sweeping the leg is done to take your opponents balance. This can be done by using the front leg to hook behind the opponents leading leg pulling it from under them or by kicking the leg out clean from under them. The student starts in the Number One Posture (Ichimonji No Kamae) with the left foot leading and raises the hands to protect the face. The students performs a powerful low kick with the right leg driving it through the back the opponents leading leg taking their balance. Alternatively the student kicks in behind the opponents leading leg and uses the foot to pull the opponents leg away, This is commonly seen in Kendo (Japanese Sports Sword Fighting) where the defender sweeps the opponents leg out from under them when they are stepping forwards to attack.

Knee Strikes - Sokki Ken

Using the hard bone parts of the knee to strike the opponent. Knee Strikes are a valuable addition to your arsenal and can be used in a wide variety of ways. There are two main ways of striking with the knees, Straight Knee Strikes and Side Knee Strikes. Straight Knee Strikes are used when striking to the groin, chest or face for example in a clinch. Side Knee Strikes are used when grappling with an opponent and attacking to the legs, ribs and face. The student starts in the Number One Posture (Ichimonji No Kamae) with the left foot leading and brings the hands up into a guard in front of the face. The student then moves forwards and strikes powerfully with the right knee. Knee Strikes (Sokki Ken) are particularly useful as additional strikes when performing locks and throws.

4 Ways Of Leaping - Shi Ho Tenchi Tobi

This time avoiding rubber Shuriken thrown by an partner (Uke).

High And Low Jump - Hicho Tobi

Jumping High or Low to cover distance to avoid low attacks (Ashi Barai) from Shinai or Bo.

3 Spirit Forms - San Shin No Kata

Earth Form - Chi No Kata
3 finger strike (San Shi Tan Ken) to pressure point in the neck. The student starts in Shizen No Kamae, then assumes Soshin No Kamae stepping straight back. The students rear hand drops down and swings straight back to an approximate 45 degree angle to the body. The student steps through with the rear leg and swings the arm up in a manner similar to a

69

pendulum striking with a 3 finger strike (San Shi Tan Ken) to the carotid artery in the neck. This can then be followed up by stepping through and striking with a secondary San Shi Tan Ken with the left hand. It is important to focus on body posture, footwork and big movements.

Water Form - Sui No Kata
The student starts is Soshin No Kamae and performs a high block followed by outside Karate chop (Omote Kiten Ken) to the neck.

The student starts in Shizen No Kamae and then assumes Soshin No Kamae stepping back at 45 degrees and assuming a low posture. A high block (Jodan Uke)i is performed with the forehand whilst simultaneously assuming Dokko No Kamae and stepping through with an outside Karate chop (Omote Kiten Ken) strike to the neck. The key point to remember with Sui No Kata is to utilize the energy generated from the twisting motion of the hips when striking and to concentrate on proper footwork and guarding the head in Dokko No Kamae.

Practice the form until it feels smooth and natural on both sides when striking. Start off slowly and then gradually speed it up and remember "If you can't do it slow, You can't do it fast!"

Fire Form - Ka No Kata
The student starts in Shizen No Kamae and then assumes Soshin No Kamae stepping back at 45 degrees and assuming a low defensive posture. Tori performs a High Block (Jodan Uke), assumes Dokko No Kamae and steps through with an Inside Karate Chop (Kiten Ken) strike to the opponents neck. The key point to remember is to utilize Taijutsu and drop the bodyweight down when the strike makes contact with the Ukes neck.

Wind Form - Fu No Kata
The student starts in a standing position (Shizen No Kamae) and then assumes Soshin No Kamae stepping back at a 45 degree angle with the right foot and dropping into a low posture. The student performs a low block (Gedan Uke) in a circular manner and proceeds to step back in towards opponent with the right foot. The student then steps straight back with the left foot and performs a Thumb Driving Fist (Shito Ken) strike to the ribs/hips utilizing the twisting motion of the hips and effective body movement. The student should move in a semi circular manner when performing the strike really driving it into the opponents ribs (Butsumetsu).

Void Form - Ku No Kata
The student starts in a standing position (Shizen No Kamae) and then assumes Soshin No Kamae stepping back at a 45 degree angle with the right foot (Ushiro Naname) and dropping into a low posture. The student performs a low block (Gedan Uke) in a circular manner with the left hand and raises the right hand high to distract the opponent. The student then performs a Forward Stamp Kick (Zenpo Geri) with the right foot forcing the opponent backwards. It's important that you throw the hand up in the air as you block the incoming attack. There are some dojos that throw the hand forwards instead of upwards but Soke and the Daishihan demonstrate it by throwing the hand upwards holding a mirror or weapon to distract the opponent.

Fundamental 8 Kata - Kihon Happo No Kata
3 Fundamental Kata - Kihon Koshi Sanpo

Number One Kata - Ichimonji No Kata

The student performs a High Block (Jodan Uke) stepping off at

45 degrees (Ushiro Naname) followed by Outside Karate Chop (Omote Kiten Ken) to the opponents neck. Remember the 3 stances Ichimonji No Kamae, Dokko No Kamae and Ichimonji No Kamae when doing the Kata. The point of the Number One Kata (Ichimonji No Kata) is to push through the opponent and take their balance by bending their spine backwards.

Cross Stance Form - Jumonji No Kata
The opponent punches with the right hand towards the students face. The student steps back at 45 degrees (Ushiro Naname) and performs a High Block (Jodan Uke) followed by a Thumb Drive Fist (Shito Ken) to armpit pressure point (Kyusho) of the opponents attacking arm and assuming Covering Eyes Posture (Kosei No Kamae). The opponent punches with the left hand a the student repeats the form stepping back at 45 degrees (Ushiro Naname) and performing a High Block (Jodan Uke) followed by a Thumb Drive Fist (Shito Ken) to the armpit pressure point of the opponents attacking arm and assuming Covering Eyes Posture (Kosei No Kamae) covering the opponents eyes. Its important to step in a zig zag motion when performing the Kata and force the opponent back when thrusting forwards with the Thumb Drive Fist (Shito Ken).

One Legged Number One Form - Hicho No Kata
The opponent punches with the right hand towards the students stomach (Chudan Tsuki). The student responds by assuming the One Legged Number One Posture (Hicho No Kamae) and performing a Low Block (Gedan Uke). The student then kicks with the left leg into the opponents armpit and strikes with an inside Karate Chop (Ura Kiten Ken) to the opponents neck. It's important to get low so that you maintain your balance when performing the block and the kick.

Defence Against Throws - Nage Kaeshi

False Punch - Okyo
The opponent attempts a throw (Outside Hip Throw - Osoto Gake). The student drops his hips for stability (Koshi Kudaki) and counters with a left Thumb Drive Fist (Shito Ken) thumb to the kidney followed by a right Fudo Ken punch to the solar plexus from the Ukes right side.

Note: A common Henka is to use an Elbow Strike (Shuki Ken) to the solar plexus (Suigetsu - Kyusho) after the Fudo Ken to slam the Uke onto his back.

Capture the Head - Zu Dori
The opponent attempts a throw (Outside Hip Throw - Osoto Gake). The student drops his hips for stability (Koshi Kudaki) and counters from the right side of the opponents body with a right punch (Migi Fudo Ken) to the face and a left hair grab at the back of the opponents head to drag him backwards and down onto the ground.

Note: A Henka of this technique is to substitute the hair grab for a Shako Ken raking into the eyes/nose to pull opponents head back and bring him to the ground.

Tip By Wind - Fu Kan
The opponent attempts a throw (Outside Hip Throw - Osoto Gake). The student punches the opponent in the face with a right Fudo Ken and grabs the the opponents shoulder with his left hand. The student then leans forward and grabs the inside of the opponents leg with the right hand. The student performs a sideways roll, dragging the opponent with him. When the opponent lands on his back the student continues to roll sitting astride the opponent to follow up with another attack.

73

Crazy Snow - Ransetsu

The opponent grabs the student by both lapels. The student grabs the sides of the opponents jacket and drives the tips of his thumbs into the opponents ribs while pulling him forwards. The student then drops to his seat sliding both of his legs between (Tachi Nagare) or off to one side (Yoko Nagare) of the opponents legs while pulling the opponent forwards and down onto his face.

Note: It is important to make sure that student sits in the space directly in between the opponents feet, If the hips aren't positioned here the opponent will likely bend his knees landing directly on the students groin. Place the hips to far back and you run the risk of the opponent mounting you so the placement of the hips is key!

Wrist Escapes - Te Hodoki

Katate Te Hodoki - Single Handed Escapes

Inside Wrist Lock Wrist Escape - Ura Gyaku Te Hodoki

The opponent grabs the students left wrist with the right hand (Straight Grab). The student responds by pinning the opponents hand in place with the right hand and turning the arm in a clockwise direction. The student grabs the opponents right hand and releases the left hand from his grip moving it up to the back of the opponents arm just above the elbow (Tricep Muscle). The student bars the opponents arm locking the wrist and increasing the angle of the arm to bring the opponent down onto the ground. It's important to bring the opponents arm into the waist to control it, close the gap when performing the lock or they may try to escape.

Tai Hodoki - Body Escapes

Cross Arm Throw Body Escape - Sakketsu

The opponent grabs the student from behind pinning both arms. The student responds by bringing the hands up between their body and the opponents arms. The student then does a backwards headbutt (Ushiro Kikaku Ken) and pushes the hips backwards whilst pushing the hands forwards breaking the opponents grasp. The student then grabs both of the opponents wrists and brings the right arm over the left crossing the opponents arms locking the elbow of the right arm. The student then raises the left arm whilst pulling down on the right arm and throws the opponent onto the ground. The arm positioning with the Cross Arm Throw Body Escape (Sakketsu) is important, you need to lock the elbow and twist the arms so that the opponent has no choice but to throw themselves over onto their back.

Aruki - Walking

Shinobi Aruki With Shuriken - Ninja Walk Throwing Shuriken.

Ninja Walk but whilst throwing Hira Shuriken (Ninja Stars) from the hip. It's important when throwing Hira Shuriken that you fully extend and spin the Shuriken a bit like throwing a frisbee. The student holds a stack of Hira Shuriken (Ninja Stars) in the left hand and performs the Ninja Walk (Shinobi Aruki). As the student steps out they extend their body leaning forwards throwing the Hira Shuriken at the target. This will be demonstrated during lessons and only rubber stars are to be used when training in the dojo.

Shurikenjutsu – Blade Throwing Art

Shurikenjutsu is the art of throwing projectile weapons like throwing stars or spikes which we call Hira Shuriken/Senban Shuriken (Stars) or Bo Shuriken (Spikes).

Shuriken translates as "Hidden Hand Blade" and are a form of Kakushi Buki – Concealed Weapon.

Practising Shurikenjutsu is not something that should be done at home and should only ever be practised in the dojo under the supervision of qualified and insured Ninjutsu instructor.

This is something that is exclusively practised in Ninjutsu or in traditional Japanese Sogo-Bugei or comprehensive Japanese martial arts systems.

Senban Shuriken - Into Nets From Standing

Throwing rubber Senban Shuriken into nets or a bucket. The important thing to remember is to spin the Shuriken when you throw it and control the direction of your throw using your Stance (Kamae). This will be explained and demonstrated during lessons.

Bo Shuriken - Into Paper/Cardboard From Standing

Throwing wooden Bo Shuriken (Spikes) into paper or cardboard targets. This is done by aiming in the Number One Posture (Ichimonji No Kamae), assuming Dokko No Kamae and then stepping through to throw the Shuriken. This will be explained and demonstrated during lessons. The Bo Shuriken will rotate during flight by 180 degrees every 6ft. 3 Ways of throwing.

Intermediate Attacking Forms - Kogeki Kata

At this point in your training you should be practising at home and looking at how to apply the techniques you have learned so far in a realistic way which means learning to attack. For your Green Belt grading we want to see 3 intermediate level combos demonstrated on the bags, a list of some potential attacking combinations we call the Kogeki Kata (Attacking Forms) can be found on page 19. I have listed 3 simple combinations for you to practice below:

- **Left Punch, Right Elbow Strike, Right Punch, Left Elbow Strike.**

- **Right Punch, Left Punch, Right Front Stamp Kick, Left Front Stamp Kick.**

- **High Block, Grab, Knee Strike, Knee Strike, Front Stamp Kick.**

Blue Belt - 4th Kyu

Stances - Kamae

Metal Hands Stance- Rushiyo No Kamae

Metal Hands Leaning Forwards - Rushiyo Fussets No Kamae

Kicks – Keri

Hidden Kick - Kakushi Keri

Heavy Low Leg Kick – Ashi Barai Keri

Pinning The Opponents Foot – Te Dama Dori

Natural Kick - Sanshin Keri

8 Ways Of Kicking – Happo Geri

Blocking – Uke Negashi

To Crush The Fist – Ken Kudaki

To Crush The Kick - Keri Kudaki

4 Ways Of Leaping - Shi Ho Tenchi Tobi

Wrist Escapes - Te Hodoki

Body Escapes - Tai Hodoki

5 Elemental Forms - San Shin No Kata

Fundamental 8 Forms - Kihon Happo No Kata

Outer Wrist Twist With Control - Omote Gyaku

Outer Wrist Twist Defending A Punch - Omote Gyaku Tskui

Bokken - Wooden Sword - *Kenjutsu*

Hasso No Kamae

Ryusui No Kamae

Kocho / Kasumi No Kamae

Iaijutsu

Nuki Uchi - Side Cut To Head Height

Shomen Uchi - Top Cut To Head Height

Gyaku Kessabattou - Under Cut To Groin Height

16 Fighting Fists - Hoken Juroppo

Headbutt - Kikaku Ken \ Zu Tsuki

Elbow Strike - Shuki Ken

Immovable Fist - Fudo Ken \ Kongo Ken

Wake Up Rolling Strike / Karate Chop - Kiten Ken \ Shuto

Finger Needle Strike - Shishin Ken

Finger Tip Strike - Shitan Ken

Jutaijutsu - Grappling

As per previous grading plus

Seoi Nage - Shoulder Throw

Tai Otoshi - Body Throw

Shinobi Aruki - Ninja Walk

Shurikenjutsu

As per previous grading plus:

Avoiding plastic Senban shuriken with various Kaiten (Rolls).

Intermediate Level of the Kogeki Kata - Striking Forms

Togakure Ryu Senban Hira Shuriken

Kicks - Keri

Hidden Kick - Kakushi Keri

The Hidden Kick (Kakushi Keri) is performed in a similar manner to Checking (Sokuyaku Suihei Keri) but this time the student kicks out the opposing leg to take the opponents balance. The student starts in a Standing Posture (Shizen No Kamae) and the opponent grabs them at chest height. The student responds by stepping back with the right foot to pull the opponent forwards. The student then kicks into the back of the opponents knee by crossing the right leg across the front of the left and stepping through to collapse the opponents leg. The student then drags the opponents off balance. This is a stamp kick where the legs cross making it quite hard to see.

Heavy Low Leg Kick - Ashi Barai Keri

The Heavy Low Leg Kick (Ashi Barai Keri) is similar to a low roundhouse and is often seen in Thai Boxing. The student starts in the Number One Posture (Ichimonji No Kamae) with the left foot leading. The student swings the right leg engaging the hips and performs a powerful Heavy Low Leg Kick (Ashi Barai Ken) to the lower part of the opponents leading leg. This differs to Sweeping The Leg (Sokuyaku Barai Keri) as the Heavy Low Leg Kick (Ashi Barai Keri) is done solely to damage the opponents leg preventing them from being able to continue the attack.

Pinning The Opponents Foot - Te Dama Dori

The students steps on the opponents leading foot pinning it to the ground and pushes them backwards so that they lose their balance and fall. Simple but extremely effective!

Natural Kick - Sanshin Keri

The Natural Kick (Sanshin Keri) is kicking in a natural way like kicking a football. The student is in a Natural Standing Posture (Shizen No Kamae) and the opponent approaches and attempts a chest grab. The student responds with a Natural Kick (Sanshin Keri) to the groin (Suzu) knocking the opponent back. This is one of the most useful kicks you can do!

8 Ways Of Kicking - Happo Geri

The 8 Ways Of Kicking (Happo Geri) are various ways of kicking the opponents legs to take their balance when you are grappling.

- **Right Sokuyaku** stamp kick to the left thigh
- **Left Sokuyaku** stamp kick to the right thigh
- **Right Sokuyaku** inward swinging kick to the outside of the left thigh.
- **Left Sokuyaku** inward swinging kick to the outside of the right thigh.
- Groin kick by swinging **Right Sokugyaku Ken** (Ball of Foot) Kick up.
- Groing kick by swinging **Left Sokugyaku Ken** (Ball of Foot) Kick up.
- **Free Kicking Method** but a Hidden Kick (Kakushi Keri) to the right leg.
- **Free Kicking Method** but a Hidden Kick (Kakushi Keri) to the left leg.

<u>Blocking</u> - Uke Negashi

To Crush The Fist - Ken Kudaki

This is blocking and then immediately striking the opponents arm with a Hammer Fist (Tetsui Fudo Ken) from the other hand. The student is stood in the Number One Posture (Ichimonji No Kamae) and the opponent punches with the right hand. The student responds by blocking with a Left High Block (Hidari Jodan Uke) and immediately strikes the opponents arm down with a Hammer Fist to the radial nerve opening the opponents guard making them vulnerable to follow up attacks. You can also forcefully knock the opponents arm out to the side to fully open their guard or just use it to check the incoming attack such as in Empty Space (Koku) where you don't want to open the opponents guard but force them into a position where they only have one possible attack.

To Crush The Kick - Keri Kudaki

This is blocking an incoming kick with with a mid level block (Chudan Uke) and punching into the vulnerable parts of the leg with the other hand. The student is stood in a Natural Standing Posture (Shizen No Kamae) and the opponent kicks with a Forward Stamp Kick (Zenpo Geri). The student steps to the outside (Omote) of the kick and blocks with a right mid level block (Migi Chudan Uke). The student then immediately punches with the left hand to the pressure point just above the knee (Usai) forcing the opponents leg away. You can also perform To Crush The Kick (Keri Kudaki) on the inside (Ura) of an incoming kick from an opponent. There is a variation of Keri Kudaki where the student uses the leading leg to guide the incoming kick past and then performs the punch to the knee (Usai) but your timing has to be perfect.

3 Spirit Forms - San Shin No Kata

Earth Form - Chi No Kata
3 finger strike (San Shi Tan Ken) to pressure point in the neck. The student starts in Shizen No Kamae, then assumes Soshin No Kamae stepping straight back. The students rear hand drops down and swings straight back to an approximate 45 degree angle to the body. The student steps through with the rear leg and swings the arm up in a manner similar to a pendulum striking with a 3 finger strike (San Shi Tan Ken) to the carotid artery in the neck. This can then be followed up by stepping through and striking with a secondary San Shi Tan Ken with the left hand. It is important to focus on body posture, footwork and big movements.

Water Form - Sui No Kata
The student starts is Soshin No Kamae and performs a high block followed by outside Karate chop (Omote Kiten Ken) to the neck.

The student starts in Shizen No Kamae and then assumes Soshin No Kamae stepping back at 45 degrees and assuming a low posture. A high block (Jodan Uke)i is performed with the forehand whilst simultaneously assuming Dokko No Kamae and stepping through with an outside Karate chop (Omote Kiten Ken) strike to the neck. The key point to remember with Sui No Kata is to utilize the energy generated from the twisting motion of the hips when striking and to concentrate on proper footwork and guarding the head in Dokko No Kamae.

Practice the form until it feels smooth and natural on both sides when striking. Start off slowly and then gradually speed it up and remember "If you can't do it slow, You can't do it fast!"

Fire Form - Ka No Kata
The student starts in Shizen No Kamae and then assumes
Soshin No Kamae stepping back at 45 degrees and assuming
a low defensive posture. Tori performs a High Block (Jodan
Uke), assumes Dokko No Kamae and steps through with an
Inside Karate Chop (Kiten Ken) strike to the opponents neck.
The key point to remember is to utilize Taijutsu and drop the
bodyweight down when the strike makes contact with the Ukes
neck.

Wind Form - Fu No Kata
The student starts in a standing position (Shizen No Kamae)
and then assumes Soshin No Kamae stepping back at a 45
degree angle with the right foot and dropping into a low
posture. The student performs a low block (Gedan Uke) in a
circular manner and proceeds to step back in towards
opponent with the right foot. The student then steps straight
back with the left foot and performs a Thumb Driving Fist
(Shito Ken) strike to the ribs/hips utilizing the twisting motion of
the hips and effective body movement. The student should
move in a semi circular manner when performing the strike
really driving it into the opponents ribs (Butsumetsu).

Void Form - Ku No Kata
The student starts in a standing position (Shizen No Kamae)
and then assumes Soshin No Kamae stepping back at a 45
degree angle with the right foot (Ushiro Naname) and dropping
into a low posture. The student performs a low block (Gedan
Uke) in a circular manner with the left hand and raises the right
hand high to distract the opponent. The student then performs
a Forward Stamp Kick (Zenpo Geri) with the right foot forcing
the opponent backwards. It's important that you throw the hand
up in the air as you block the incoming attack. There are some
dojos that throw the hand forwards instead of upwards but

Soke and the Daishihan demonstrate it by throwing the hand upwards holding a mirror or weapon to distract the opponent.

Fundamental 8 Kata - Kihon Happo No Kata
3 Fundamental Kata - Kihon Koshi Sanpo

Number One Kata - Ichimonji No Kata

The student performs a High Block (Jodan Uke) stepping off at 45 degrees (Ushiro Naname) followed by Outside Karate Chop (Omote Kiten Ken) to the opponents neck. Remember the 3 stances Ichimonji No Kamae, Dokko No Kamae and Ichimonji No Kamae when doing the Kata. The point of the Number One Kata (Ichimonji No Kata) is to push through the opponent and take their balance by bending their spine backwards.

Cross Stance Form - Jumonji No Kata

The opponent punches with the right hand towards the students face. The student steps back at 45 degrees (Ushiro Naname) and performs a High Block (Jodan Uke) followed by a Thumb Drive Fist (Shito Ken) to armpit pressure point (Kyusho) of the opponents attacking arm and assuming Covering Eyes Posture (Kosei No Kamae). The opponent punches with the left hand a the student repeats the form stepping back at 45 degrees (Ushiro Naname) and performing a High Block (Jodan Uke) followed by a Thumb Drive Fist (Shito Ken) to the armpit pressure point of the opponents attacking arm and assuming Covering Eyes Posture (Kosei No Kamae) covering the opponents eyes. Its important to step in a zig zag motion when performing the Kata and force the opponent back when thrusting forwards with the Thumb Drive Fist (Shito Ken).

One Legged Number One Form - Hicho No Kata
The opponent punches with the right hand towards the students stomach (Chudan Tsuki). The student responds by assuming the One Legged Number One Posture (Hicho No Kamae) and performing a Low Block (Gedan Uke). The student then kicks with the left leg into the opponents armpit and strikes with an inside Karate Chop (Ura Kiten Ken) to the opponents neck. It's important to get low so that you maintain your balance when performing the block and the kick.

Five Forms - Toride Kihon Kata Go Ho

Outer Wrist Twist - Omote Gyaku
The opponents right hand is gripped by both of students hands turning the opponents hand so that his palm is facing towards him and the fingers pointing upwards. The student then steps in with his right leg and back with his left whilst pushing opponents hand towards the forearm and twisting the wrist to the left at the same time causing the opponent to land on his back. Ensure that you do not turn your back on the opponent when applying the lock and drive the knuckle of opponents little finger down towards the ground.

Outer Wrist Twist Against Punch - Omote Gyaku Tsuki
The opponent grabs the students jacket with the left hand and steps in with the right leg to punch (Fudo Ken) with the right hand to the students face. The student covers the opponents grabbing hand with the right hand while in Shizen No Kamae, then as the the opponent steps in to punch (Fudo Ken)the the student steps back and performs High Block (Jodan Uke) to parry away the opponents punch (Fudo Ken). The student then grips the left hand of the opponent and side steps (Yoko Aruki) to a 90 degree angle as if taking the opponent into Inside Arm Lock (Ura Gyaku). It is important to maintain pressure on the

opponents elbow with the students forearm as the side step (Yoko Aruki) is performed to ensure the opponents balance is tipped forward and the student is clear of any potential attacks that the opponent might attempt. The student then steps off line, slightly behind the opponent and performs Outer Wrist Twist (Omote Gyaku) pushing down on the knuckle of the little finger as opposed to twisting the wrist horizontally.

Note: By pushing down on the knuckle of the little finger I mean when twisting the hand for Ourt Wrist Twist (Omote Gyaku) you force the arm in towards the opponents body and the knuckle down towards the floor.

16 Fighting Fists – Hoken Juroppo

The 16 Fighting Fists (Hoken Juroppo) are various hand positions used for striking. The full list can be found on page 17 but you are required to know the ones below for Blue Belt.

Headbutt - Kikaku Ken \ Zu Tsuki
Using the thick bone areas of the forehead, sides, and back of the head in smashing or butting actions. This is not your typical headbutt where you swing your head forwards (Glasgow Kiss) but more like standing up under the opponents chin while supporting the neck with the shoulders.

Elbow Strike - Shuki Ken
Using the muscles in the forearms and bone points of the elbows to strike close targets. The students assumes the Number One Posture (Ichimonji No Kamae) with the left foot leading. The student steps through with the right leg and raises the right arm to chest level with the palm facing towards the opponent. The student then strikes the opponent in the face

with the forearm using the twisting motion of the hips to drive it through.

Immovable Fist - Fudo Ken \ Kongo Ken
Using the clenched fist for punching or striking. There are various ways of performing the Immovable Fist (Fudo Ken) and entire arts such as Boxing based solely on punching. The student starts in the Number One Posture (Ichimonji No Kamae) with the left foot leading. The student then steps through with the right foot and performs a straight punch to the opponents face with the right hand. The student then steps through with the left foot and punches with the left hand to the opponents face finishing in the Number One Posture (Ichimonji No Kamae). The above is just a basic example however you can also Jab, Cross, Hook, Uppercut (Sake Choiyaku Tsuki) and Hammer Fit (Tetsui Fudo Ken) in various combinations like in the Kogeki Kata..

Wake Up Rolling Strike / Karate Chop - Kiten Ken \ Shuto
Snapping the hand open at the point of impact, to strike with the outer edge of the palm. The student starts in the Number One Posture (Ichimonji No Kamae) with the left foot leading. The student then takes a slight step diagonally backwards (Ushiro Naname) and assumes One Line With Rear Arm Guarding Head (Dokko No Kamae). The student then steps forwards with the right foot and strikes with an outside Karate Chop (Kiten Ken) to the opponents neck finishing in Number One Posture (Ichimonji No Kamae). You can also perform the Karate Chop (Kiten Ken) to the inside of the opponents neck.

Finger Needle Strike - Shishin Ken
Using any individual fingertips for poking or applying pressure such as poking the opponent in the eye or pushing a finger into a pressure point (Kyusho). This is not for striking!

Finger Tip Strike - Shitan Ken
Using three or four fingertips together in a thrusting motion like in the Earth Form (Chi No Kata) from the 3 Spirit Forms (Sanshin No Kata). Using three fingers is called San Shitan Ken, Four is Yon Shitan Ken and five is Go Shitan Ken. Again this strike is mainly for thrusting into pressure points or soft tissue such as the opponents throat.

Grappling - Jutaijutsu

Shoulder Throw - Seoi Nage
The student starts in a Natural Standing Posture (Shizen No Kamae) and the opponent punches with the right hand towards the students face. The student responds by assuming the Number One Posture (Ichimonji No Kamae) and blocking with a High Block (Jodan Uke) with the left hand. The student grabs the opponents wrist with the left hand and steps in with the right foot bringing the right shoulder under the opponents right armpit. The student then grabs the opponents arm with the right hand and pulls it forwards closing the gap between the student and the opponent. The student then bends the knees and straightens the legs lifting the opponent on the shoulder and throws them onto their back by dragging them around the right side of the body. Do not throw them over your shoulder onto their head!

Body Throw - Tai Otoshi
Using the hips to lift the opponent and throw them to the ground. The student grabs the opponents right sleeve with his left hand and left lapel with his right hand (Kumi Uchi). The student then steps into the opponents space and positions his hips in front of the opponents, bending the knees to lift the opponent onto the students hips. The student then pulls the opponent around his body and lifts his hips to unbalance and

90

throw the opponent onto the ground. It's important to keep the right arm vertically against the opponents chest to drag them round into the throw.

Swordsmanship - Kenjutsu - *Bokken*

Stances - Kamae

Hasso No Kamae

Ryusui No Kamae

Kocho / Kasumi No Kamae

Sword Drawing - Iaijutsu

Side Cut To Head Height - Nuki Uchi

Drawing the sword and cutting horizontally in one fluid motion. The student starts in a Natural Standing Posture (Shizen No Kamae) with the sword in their Obi (Belt). The student pushes on the hand guard (Tsuba) with the thumb of the left hand and brings the right hand into position on the handle with the knuckles pointing upwards. The student begins to draw the sword out of the sheath (Saya) and once its two thirds of the way out turns the sword and sheath so that the blade faces to the left. The student draws the sheath back and cuts horizontally to the right stopping once the tip (Kissaki) is in line with the students right shoulder. Make sure that the thumb of the left hand is clear and doesn't go near the sharp edge of the blade when drawing as its a bad habit that could lead to the student cutting themselves with a real sword (Katana).

Top Cut To Head Height - Shomen Uchi

The student starts in a Natural Standing Posture (Shizen No Kamae) with the sword in their Obi (Belt). The student pushes on the hand guard (Tsuba) with the thumb of the left hand and brings the right hand into position on the handle with the knuckles pointing upwards. The student begins to draw the sword out of the sheath (Saya) and once its two thirds of the way out pulls the sheath (Saya) back and cuts vertically downwards to the top of the opponents head (Shomen Uchi). The cuts should stop at the belly button, don't follow through with the cut pointing the tip (Kissaki) towards the ground. Make sure that the thumb of the left hand is clear and doesn't go near the sharp edge of the blade when drawing as its a bad habit that could lead to the student cutting themselves with a real sword (Katana).

Under Cut To Groin Height - Gyaku Kessabattou

Drawing the sword and cutting horizontally in one fluid motion. The student starts in a Natural Standing Posture (Shizen No Kamae) with the sword in their Obi (Belt). The student pushes on the hand guard (Tsuba) with the thumb of the left hand and brings the right hand into position on the handle with the knuckles pointing upwards. The student begins to draw the sword out of the sheath (Saya) dropping down and once its two thirds of the way out turns the sword and sheath so that the blade faces downwards. The student draws the sheath back and cuts vertically upwards towards the hands to disarm the opponent finishing the cut just about head height with the tip (Kissaki) pointing towards the opponent. Make sure that the thumb of the left hand is clear and doesn't go near the sharp edge of the blade when drawing as its a bad habit that could lead to the student cutting themselves.

Intermediate Attacking Forms - Kogeki Kata

At this point in your training you should be practising at home and looking at how to apply the techniques you have learned so far in a realistic way which means learning to attack. For your Green Belt grading we want to see 3 intermediate level combos demonstrated on the bags, a list of some potential attacking combinations we call the Kogeki Kata (Attacking Forms) can be found on page 19. I have listed some simple combinations for you to practice below:

- Left Punch, Right Elbow Strike, Right Punch, Left Elbow Strike.

- Right Punch, Left Punch, Right Front Stamp Kick, Left Front Stamp Kick.

- High Block, Grab, Knee Strike, Knee Strike, Front Stamp Kick

- Left High Block, Right Roundhouse, Right Low Block, Front Stamp Kick.

- Punch, Punch, Roundhouse, Reversed Roundhouse, 360 Crescent Kick.

- Left High Block, Right High Block, Left Punch, Right Punch, Right Elbow Strike, Left Front Stamp Kick.

Purple Belt - 3rd Kyu

Stretching - Junan Taiso

Falling Forms - Ukemi Gata

Stances - Kamae

Kicks - Keri

4 Ways Of Leaping - Shi Ho Tenchi Tobi

Wrist Escapes - Te Hodoki

Body Escapes - Tai Hodoki

3 Spirit Forms - San Shin No Kata

Fundamental 8 Forms - Kihon Happo No Kata
Base Reversal - Hon Gyaku
Inside Wrist Twist - Ura Gyaku

Wooden Sword - Bokken
Gedan No Kamae

Jizurigedan No Kamae

Sword Drawing - Iaijutsu

8 Sword Cuts - Happo Biken

16 Fighting Fists - Hoken Juroppo

Claw - Shako Ken
Thumb Drive Fist - Shito Ken
Extended Knuckle Fist - Shikan Ken
Thumb Knuckle Fist - Koppo Ken
Eight Leaves Strike - Happa Ken
Heel Kick - Soku Yaku Ken
Knee Strike - Sokki Ken
Ball Of Foot Kick - Soku Gyaku Ken
Body Fist - Tai Ken
Natural Weapons - Shizen Ken

Joint Locks - Gyaku Waza

Breaking The Bamboo Inside - Ura Take Ori

Grappling - Jutaijutsu

Brushing The Waist - Haraigoshi

Big Outside Trap - Osoto Gake

Moving Like Flowing Water - Ryusui Iki Nagare

Side Flow - Yoko Nagare

Blade Flow - Tachi Nagare

Ninja Walk - Shinobi Aruki

Hidden Blade Throwing - Shurikenjutsu

Plastic Ninja Stars (Hira Shuriken) into nets after rolling.

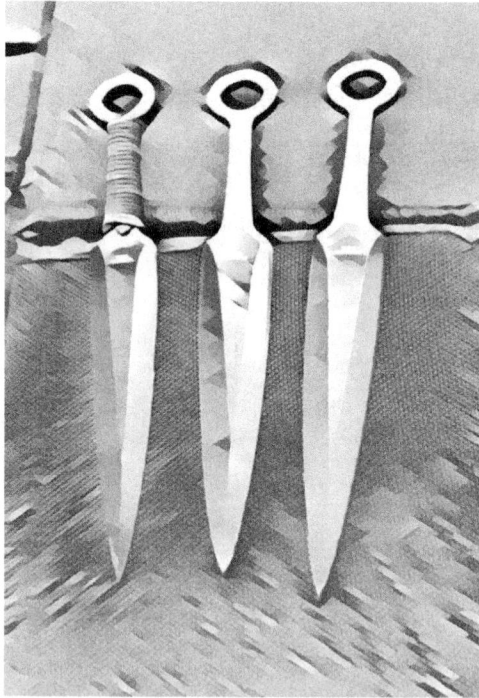

Kunai / Tantogata - Ninja Throwing Knives

Fundamental 8 Kata - Kihon Happo No Kata
Five Grabbing Forms - Toride Kihon Kata Go Ho

Base Reversal - Hon Gyaku
The opponents right hand is held in a position with the thumb down and palm edge up. The students right hand grips the opponents right hand along the back and the left hand along the palm. The student steps back with his right foot and pulls the opponent off balance while applying pressure down on the opponents straightened right wrist. The opponent drops straight down and can then be pulled on to his stomach.

Note - Hon Gyaku is part of the Gyaku Waza so its not technically part of the Kihon Happo,

Inside Wrist Twist - Ura Gyaku
The student starts in a Natural Standing Posture (Shizen No Kamae) with the opponent grabbing with the left hand. The opponents left hand is gripped across the back by the students right hand. The students left hand grips opponents left hand for support and then the student applies downward pressure to the outside of the opponents left elbow using the outer edge of the forearm to cut into the tricep muscle just above the elbow. The student steps back with the left foot whilst folding the opponents wrist and twisting the wrist in an inward anti-clockwise direction. Bring the opponent down. It is important to ensure that the students arm is brought close to the body and that there is no gap for the opponent to escape.

Swordsmanship - Kenjutsu - *Bokken*

Stances - Kamae

Gedan No Kamae

Jizurigedan No Kamae

Sword Drawing - Iaijutsu

Shield Draw - Tate Uchi

The student is stood in a Natural Standing Posture (Shizen No Kamae) with the sword (Katana). The student pushes the hand guard (Tsuba) with the thumb of the left hand to release it from the sheath and brings the right hand onto the handle (Tsuka) with the knuckles facing upwards. The student performs the Ninja Walk (Shinobi Aruki) and draws the sword up vertically on the left side to block an incoming attack. The student then fully draws the sword bringing it above the head and turns the ankles so that he they can perform a Left Diagonal Downwards Cut (Hidari Kesa Kiri) to the opponent.

8 Sword Cuts - Happo Kiri

Downwards Cut - Tento Kiri

Left Diagonal Downwards Cut - Hidari Kesa Kiri

Right Diagonal Downwards Cut - Migi Kesa Kiri

Left Horizontal Cut - Hidari Do Kiri

Right Horizontal Cut - Migi Do Kiri

Left Diagonal Upwards Cut - Hidari Gyaku Kesa Kiri

Right Diagonal Upwards Cut - Migi Gyaku Kesa Kiri

Upwards Cut - Kiri Age

Thrust - Tsuki

16 Fighting Fists – Hoken Juroppo

The 16 Fighting Fists (Hoken Juroppo) are various hand positions used for striking. The full list can be found on page 17 but you are required to know the ones below for Purple Belt (3rd Kyu).

Claw - Shako Ken

Striking with the tips of the fingers in a clawing motion. The student starts in the Number One Posture (Ichimonji No Kamae) with the left foot leading. The student steps through with the right leg and claws at the opponents face with the right hand.

Thumb Drive Fist - Shito Ken

Striking to sensitive areas of the body and pressure points (Kyusho) with the tip of the thumb extended from a fist. The student starts in the Number One Posture (Ichimonji No Kamae) with the left foot leading. The student steps through with the right foot and strikes with a Thumb Drive Fist (Shito Ken) to the opponents ribs (Butsumetsu).

Extended Knuckle Fist - Shikan Ken

Striking with the extended knuckles of the fingers to damage soft tissue and cause pain. The student starts in the Number One Posture (Ichimonji No Kamae) with the left foot leading. The opponent punches with the right hand and the student does a High Block (Jodan Uke) with the left hand and performs a Extended Knuckle Fist (Shikan Ken) to the opponents bicep muscle to drive the arm away. Similar to To Crush A Fist (Ken Kudaki).

Thumb Knuckle Fist - Koppo Ken

Using the raised knuckles of the thumbs to grab or strike to sensitive areas such as the Temple (Kasumi). The student starts in the Number One Posture (Ichimonji No Kamae) with the left foot leading. The student steps through with the right foot and grabs the opponent for a choke but uses the Thumb Knuckle Fist (Koppo Ken) to dig into the sides of the opponents neck causing pain and dragging them down to the ground.

Eight Leaves Strike - Happa Ken

Slapping the opponent with an open hand and also striking with the palm of the hand in a manner similar to punching. The student starts in the Number One Posture (Ichimonji No Kamae) with the left foot leading. The students steps through with the right leg and strikes with a Eight Leaves Strike (Happa Ken) to the opponents chin forcing them backwards.

Heel Kick - Soku Yaku Ken

The same as in the Kicks section (Keri Waza). Kicking using the heel of the foot. The student starts in the Number One Posture (Ichimonji No Kamae) with the left foot leading. The student steps through and performs a Front Stamp Kick (Zenpo Geri) striking with the heel of the foot (Soku Yaku Ken) to force the opponent back.

Knee Strike - Sokki Ken

The same as in the Kicks section (Keri Waza). Using the hard bone parts of the knee to strike the opponent. Knee Strikes are a valuable addition to your arsenal and can be used in a wide variety of ways. There are two main ways of striking with the knees, Straight Knee Strikes and Side Knee Strikes. Straight Knee Strikes are used when striking to the groin, chest or face for example in a clinch. Side Knee Strikes are used when grappling with an opponent and attacking to the legs, ribs and face. The student starts in the Number One Posture (Ichimonji No Kamae) with the left foot leading and brings the hands up into a guard in front of the face. The student then moves forwards and strikes powerfully with the right knee. Knee Strikes (Sokki Ken) are particularly useful as additional strikes when performing locks and throws.

Ball Of Foot Kick - Soku Gyaku Ken

The same as in the Kicks section (Keri Waza). Using the ball of the foot to kick the opponent. This could be in a similar way to your Front Stamp Kick or using the ball of the foot to strike like when performing a Reverse Roundhouse. Any kick where you dig in, push or strike with the ball of the foot is considered a Sokugyaku Ken.

Body Fist - Tai Ken
Using the body to strike and apply locks. The Body Fist (Tai Ken) can be as simple as shoulder barging your opponent to knock them over. The student starts in the Number One Posture (Ichimonji No Kamae) with the left foot leading. The opponent punches with the right hand and the student steps to the outside of the punch and performs a High Block (Jodan Uke) catching the opponents wrist with the right hand. The student extends out the opponents arm and performs a Body Fist (Tai Ken) to the opponents elbow (*Tsuki Gata - Koto*).

Natural Weapons - Shizen Ken

Natural weapons such as scratching, biting, pinching, etc.

Joint Locks - Gyaku Waza

Breaking The Bamboo Inside - Ura Take Ori
The opponent grabs the student at chest height with the right hand. The student responds by performing a natural kick to the groin (Suzu), grabbing the opponents hand with the left hand and pushing it to the right to get it off the students clothing. The student then grabs the back of the opponents hand with the right hand and bends the wrist inwards so that the fingers are pointing towards the opponent. The student then supports the opponents elbow with the left hand and pushes down on the opponents wrist with the right hand to apply the lock (Take Ori) bringing the opponent to the ground by turning to the left.

Grappling - Jutaijutsu

Brushing the Waist - Haraigoshi
The student uses his back and hips to throw the opponent. The students right hand grips the opponents left lapel or shoulder and the students left hand grips the opponents right arm or lapel. The student steps in turning into the opponent with the right foot positioning the hips in front opponent right leg. The opponent is pressed close to the student and body slamming is used to get the opponent into position for a throw. The student bends the knees and lifts the hips supporting the opponents weight whilst twisting the hips to throw the opponent onto his back.

Big Outside Trap - Osoto Gake
The student and opponent stand facing one another grabbing one lapel and one sleeve each (Kumi Uchi). The student lifts the opponents right arm with the left hand to create an opening and steps in with the right foot. The student positions the hips

102

slightly behind the opponents right leg, bends the knees and straightens the legs to slightly lift the opponent with the hips. The student then pulls on the opponents right arm with the left hand and lifts their lapel with the right hand to throw them onto the ground. If the opponent steps back when the student attempts the throw simply perform a Hook Kick (Kagi Keri) into the back of the opponents right leg to sweep it stopping them from stepping and launching them onto their back.

Moving Like Flowing Water - Ryusui Iki Nagare

Side Flow - Yoko Nagare

The student grabs onto both of the opponents lapels and kicks both feet out to the side using the bodyweight to throw the opponent. It's important that the student lays across the opponents feet stopping them from stepping and preventing them from landing on the student. This is what they would call a Sutemi (Sacrificial Throw) in Judo as your sacrificing your position to be able to throw the opponent.

Blade Flow - Tachi Nagare

The students grabs onto both of the opponents lapels and slides both feet in between the opponents legs sitting in between his feet. The student uses the dropping and sliding action to counter balance the opponent and throw them onto their face. Make sure that you sit in between the opponents feet as if you sit in front of the opponent they will land on top of you

Hidden Blade Throwing - Shurikenjutsu

Throwing plastic Ninja Stars (Hira Shuriken) into nets after rolling in various directions.

103

<u>Brown Belt</u> - 2nd kyu

Stretching - Junan Taiso

Falling Forms - Ukemi Gata

Stances - Kamae

Kicks - Keri

4 Ways Of Leaping - Shi Ho Tenchi Tobi

Wrist Escapes - Te Hodoki

Body Escapes - Tai Hodoki

3 Spirit Forms - San Shin No Kata
Henka with Bokken

Swordsmanship – Kenjutsu - *Bokken*
Ichi No Kamae
Chudan No Kamae
Ryusui No Kamae
Totoku Hyoshi No Kamae

Fundamental 8 Forms - Kihon Happo No Kata
With Control - Musha Dori
Rock Throw - Ganseki Nage

Joint Locks - Gyaku Waza
Breaking The Bamboo Outside - Omote Take Ori
Crushing The Demon Outside - Omote Oni Kudaki
Crushing The Demon Inside - Ura Oni Kudaki
Big Twist - O Gyaku

Grappling - Jutaijutsu
Uchimata Uchigake
Ho Teki

Throws - Nage Waza
Irimi Nage
Ganseki Otoshi
Gyaku Nage

Ryusui Iki Nagare - Moving \like Flowing Water
Tomoe Nagare
Kuruma Nagare

Shinobi Aruki - Ninja Walk

Shurikenjutsu - Hidden Blade Throwing
Use of shuriken in grappling.

Advanced Level of the Kogeki Kata - Advanced Striking Forms

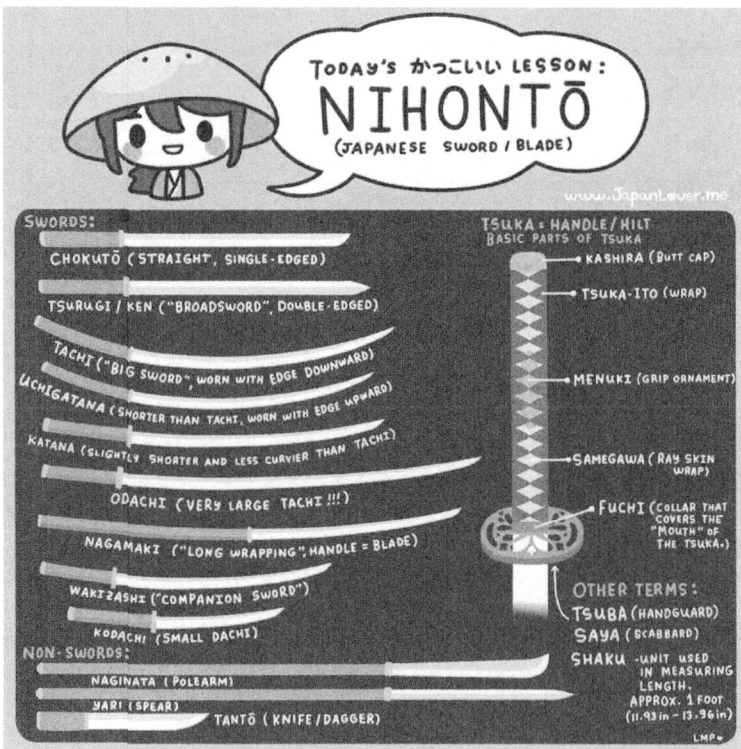

TODAY'S かっこいい LESSON:
NIHONTŌ
(JAPANESE SWORD / BLADE)

www.JapanLover.me

SWORDS:

CHOKUTŌ (STRAIGHT, SINGLE-EDGED)

TSURUGI / KEN ("BROADSWORD", DOUBLE-EDGED)

TACHI ("BIG SWORD", WORN WITH EDGE DOWNWARD)

UCHIGATANA (SHORTER THAN TACHI, WORN WITH EDGE UPWARD)

KATANA (SLIGHTLY SHORTER AND LESS CURVIER THAN TACHI)

ODACHI (VERY LARGE TACHI !!!)

NAGAMAKI ("LONG WRAPPING", HANDLE = BLADE)

WAKIZASHI ("COMPANION SWORD")

KODACHI (SMALL DACHI)

NON-SWORDS:

NAGINATA (POLEARM)

YARI (SPEAR)

TANTŌ (KNIFE/DAGGER)

TSUKA = HANDLE/HILT
BASIC PARTS OF TSUKA

• KASHIRA (BUTT CAP)

• TSUKA-ITO (WRAP)

• MENUKI (GRIP ORNAMENT)

• SAMEGAWA (RAY SKIN WRAP)

• FUCHI (COLLAR THAT COVERS THE "MOUTH" OF THE TSUKA.)

OTHER TERMS:
TSUBA (HANDGUARD)
SAYA (SCABBARD)
SHAKU -UNIT USED IN MEASURING LENGTH. APPROX. 1 FOOT (11.93in - 13.96in)

LMP♥

3 Spirit Forms - San Shin No Kata
Variation (Henka) With A Sword (Bokken)

Earth Form With Bokken - Chi No Kata

Two diagonal upward robe cuts (Kiri Age).

Water Form With Bokken - Sui No Kata

Two diagonal downward robe cuts (Kesa Kiri).

Fire Form With Bokken - Ka No Kata

High block (Jodan Uke), Inside robe cut (Kesa Kiri).

Wind Form With Bokken - Fu No Kata

Low block (Gedan Uke), Lunge (Tsuki).

Void Form With Bokken - Ku No Kata

Low block (Gedan Uke), Kick (Zenpo Geri) lifting the sword high, Cut straight down (Tento Kiri).

Bokken – Wooden Sword

Ichi No Kamae

Chudan No Kamae

Ryusui No Kamae

Totoku Hyoshi No Kamae

Fundamental 8 Kata - Kihon Happo No Kata
Five Forms - Toride Kihon Kata Go Ho

Capture The Warrior - Musha Dori

The opponent grabs students right sleeve with his left hand.

The student pulls his right hand back while stepping forward with his left foot.
The student steps forward with his right foot while reaching over the opponents left elbow with his right hand bringing it down along the outside of the opponents body and then under the left elbow while bending the knees and dropping the body weight to take the opponents balance.
The left hand then supports the right and pushes up lifting the opponents folded elbow in an inward direction to manipulate opponents shoulder and take their balance.

Rock Throw - Ganseki Nage
The students stands in front of the opponent with his right side pressed against the opponents left side.
The students right arm moves under and behind the opponents left shoulder with the palm of the students right hand pointing forward above the opponents left shoulder, do not grab opponents Shoulder.

Without bending forward, the student twists his hips and shoulders to his left to throw the opponent onto the ground by taking his balance.

Think of performing the Rock Throw (Ganseki Nage) like throwing a ball to the left over the opponents left shoulder or alternatively bring the right hand down to the students left knee dropping the opponent flat onto their face.

Joint Locks - Gyaku Waza

Breaking The Bamboo Outside - Omote Take Ori

The student starts in a Natural Standing Posture (Shizen No Kamae) and the opponent grabs the students left wrist with the right hand. The student performs a clockwise circle (Te Hodoki) with the left wrist and then grabs the back of the opponents hand with the right hand. The student releases the left wrist from the opponents grip and grabs the opponents right elbow. The student bends the wrist inwards with the right hand pushing the opponents arm up vertically until they are on the tips of their toes. The student then takes a big step past the opponents right hip with the right foot dragging the locked arm down in a large arc. The student slams the opponent onto their back and continues to apply the wrist lock (Take Ori) on the ground. If the opponent starts to step sweep the right leg out with a Hook Kick (Kagi Keri) taking the opponents balance.

Crushing The Demon Outside - Omote Oni Kudaki

The student starts in a Natural Standing Posture (Shizen No Kamae) and the opponent grabs the students left lapel with the right hand. The student brings the left hand up on the inside of the opponents grabbing wrist in a relaxed manner. The student then brings the right arm under the opponents right arm just above the elbow joint with the palm facing outwards. The student brings the left hand forwards to the right hand pushing the opponents arm into an L shape. The student then turns to the left pushing the opponents arm backwards locking the shoulder joint and brings the opponent down onto the ground. It's important to make sure that you don't turn the hands when bringing them together as it creates a gap to escape.

Crushing The Demon Inside - Inside Oni Kudaki

The student starts in a Natural Standing Posture (Shizen No Kamae) and the opponent grabs the students left lapel with the right hand. The student brings the left hand up on the inside of the opponents grabbing wrist in a relaxed manner. The student then brings the right arm over the opponents right arm hooking the hand into the elbow of the students left arm. With the opponents arm in an L shape the student turns to the left while pushing the locked shoulder backwards and brings the opponent down onto the ground. This is somewhat similar to the figure 4 armlock. If the opponent steps back with the right leg when applying the lock simply sweep the leg with a Hook Kick (Kagi Keri).

Big Twist - O Gyaku

The student starts in a Natural Standing Posture (Shizen No Kamae) and the opponent grabs the students left lapel with the right hand. The student responds by grabbing the opponents right hand with the left hand and the opponents right shoulder with the right hand. The student kicks the opponent in the groin (Suzu) and pushes their arm all the way under and back until the shoulder locks with the arm pointing straight up in the air. The student then applies pressure to the opponents wrist and drags the shoulder down towards the ground while stepping back into a kneeling position with the right leg. As the student drops they drag the opponent down onto their face ready for follow up attacks. If you do the kick, step back into a kneeling position and drag the opponent down in the same motion then it become Gekkan from Shiden Fudo Ryu Dakentaijutsu which is one of the techniques in the Densho (Ninja Scrolls) past black belt (Shodan).

110

Grappling - Jutaijutsu

Leg Lifting Sweep - Uchimata Uchigake

The student uses his right leg in between the opponents legs to lift and pull, or lift and sweep the opponents left leg from the inside. The throw can pull the opponent onto his face or throw him onto his back. For example the student performs an Inside Wrist Twist (Ura Gyaku) into Leg Lefting Sweep (Uchimata Uchigake) to bring the opponent down face first on the ground.

Release and Throw - Ho Teki

The student is stood in a Natural Standing Posture (Shizen No Kamae) and the opponent grabs onto the students right lapel with the left hand. The student responds by stepping back with the right foot bringing the right hand under the opponents left elbow and stepping back in with the right foot locking the opponents elbow. The student then grabs the opponents wrist with the right hand, steps in with the left foot for a Big Outside Trap (Osoto Gake) throw and strikes into the opponents elbow with a left Hammer Fist (Tetsui Fudo Ken) whilst sweeping the opponent with a Hook Kick (Kagi Keri). The Release and Throw (Ho Teki) is all about raising the opponent up and then slamming them onto their back so it needs to be done swiftly.

Throws - Nage Waza

Entering In - Irimi Nage

Entering In (Irimi Nage) is really simple but very effective! The student starts in a Natural Standing Posture (Shizen No Kamae) and the opponent punches towards the students face with the right hand. The student steps diagonally to the left (Naname Mae Omote) and assumes a right Number One Posture (Ichimonji No Kamae) bringing the right arm under the

111

opponents punching arm and delivering a Palm Heel Strike (Happa Ken) to the chin. The left arm is in position on the right arm protecting the face. The student steps through pushing the chin up forcing the opponent onto his back. This is a quick counter to a punch you quite literally walk through the opponent.

Rock Throw With Sweep - Ganseki Otoshi

The students stands in front of the opponent with his right side pressed against the opponents left side.
The students right arm moves under and behind the opponents left shoulder with the palm of the students right hand pointing forward above the opponents left shoulder, do not grab opponents Shoulder.

Without bending forward, the student twists his hips and shoulders to his left and sweeps the opponents left leg with a Hook Kick (Kagi Keri) to throw the opponent onto the ground by taking his balance.

Think of performing the Rock Throw With Sweep (Ganseki Otoshi) like throwing a ball to the left over the opponents left shoulder or alternatively bring the right hand down to the students left knee dropping the opponent flat onto their face.

Twisting Throw - Gyaku Nage

The student is stood in a Natural Standing Posture (Shizen No Kamae) and the opponent punches towards the face with the right hand. The student steps diagonally to the left to the outside of the punch (Naname Mae Omote) and grabs the opponents wrist with the right hand. The student then turns to the right bringing the opponents outstretched arm over the left shoulder and turns it so that the palm is facing upwards. The student bends the knees pulling the arm down and then stands up locking the arm and dragging the opponent forward into the throw. Be careful when performing this technique make sure you don't put too much pressure on the elbow, position your shoulder in the opponents armpit!

Moving Like Flowing Water - Ryusui Iki Nagare

Tomoe Nagare

This is an iconic Judo throw! The student grabs the opponents lapels with both hands and drops back to his seat, rolling onto his back, whilst shoving his foot into the opponents stomach and throwing him over the students head. For the sake of safety in the dojo please allow your opponent to roll when performing this technique, It is not a competition to see how far you can launch your partner across the mats.

Kuruma Nagare

The student grabs the opponents lapels with both hands and drops back to his seat swinging his foot up into the opponents groin (Suzu) and throwing him over his head and onto his back. The student continues to flow with the technique, rolling up onto the opponents chest to apply a restraining hold or choke. It's important to flow during Kuruma Nagare doing the throw and rolling mount in one fluid motion.

Shurikenjutsu - Hidden Blade Throwing

Use of shuriken in grappling to hook, slash and poke the opponent into submission. This will be covered during lessons.

Advanced Attacking Forms - Kogeki Kata

At this point in your training you should be practising at home and looking at how to apply the techniques you have learned so far in a realistic way which means learning to attack. For your Brown Belt grading we want to see 3 advanced level combos demonstrated on the bags, a list of some potential attacking combinations we call the Kogeki Kata (Attacking Forms) can be found on page 19. I have listed some simple combinations for you to practice below:

- **Right Front Stamp Kick, Right Reversed Roundhouse, Left Roundhouse, Right Reversed Roundhouse.**

- **Left High Block, Right Palm Heel Strike, Left Punch, Right Roundhouse, Left Front Stamp Kick.**

- **Left Front Stamp Kick, Right Roundhouse, Right Reversed Roundhouse, Right Reversed Sweep.**

- **Left Crushing Block, Right Crushing Block, Right Front Stamp Kick, Left Front Stamp Kick.**

Brown Belt With Black Stripe - 1st Kyu

Body And Weapon As One - Ken Tai Ichi Jo

There is no need to rely on muscle tension alone when hitting. Just moving the body makes the punch effective. Use the entire body movement to create energy in striking.

Stretching - Junan Taiso

Falling Forms - Ukemi Gata

Stances - Kamae

Kicks - Keri

4 Ways Of Leaping - Shi Ho Tenchi Tobi

Wrist Escapes - Te Hodoki

Body Escapes - Tai Hodoki

3 Spirit Forms - San Shin No Kata

Fundamental 8 Forms - Kihon Happo No Kata

Punching Forms - Tsuki Gata
Lets Fall To Hell - Jigoku Otoshi
One Side Coil - Kata Maki

Joint Locks - Gyaku Waza
Twin Warrior Capture - Muso Dori

Grappling - Jutaijutsu

Moving Like Flowing Water - Ryusui Iki Nagare
Hand Pillow - Te Makura
Shoulder Wheel - Kata Guruma
Whirlwind Roll - Uzumaki

Grabbing Forms - Torite Waza
Inside Restraints - Ura Gatame
Outside Restraints - Omote Gatame

Actual Fighting Training - Shinken Gata Kieko
Give a Ride - Renyo
False Space - Koku

Advanced Attacking Forms - Advanced Kogeki Kata

Punching Forms - Tsuki Gata

Lets Fall To Hell - Jigoku Otoshi

The student is stood in a Natural Standing Posture (Shizen No Kamae). The opponent steps forwards with a right punch (Fudo Ken) to the students face. The student responds by sliding back and to the left in a right Number One Posture (Ichimonji No Kamae) while performing a right outside High Block (Omote Jodan Uke). The student immediately grabs the opponents wrist and and stretches the arm out in front of them. The student then uses their left knee to apply pressure to the outside of the right elbow in order to drive the opponent to the ground. Be careful when performing this technique its easy to injure your partner!

One Side Coil - Kata Maki

The student is stood in a Natural Standing Posture (Shizen No Kamae). The opponent steps in with a right punch and a left punch (Fudo Ken) directed towards the students face. The student blocks the first punch with a High Block (Jodan Uke) and then seeing the opponents left arm raise to punch again the student steps forwards with the right foot and performs Capture The Warrior (Musha Dori). The student then steps back with his right foot while driving a left Thumb Drive Fist (Shito Ken) into the opponents right ribs. The student then pivots in a clockwise direction dropping to a kneeling position on the right knee to pull the opponent backwards and down onto the ground. Be careful when performing One Side Coil (Kata Maki), Don't do it fast you could hurt your partner quite easily if you do the lock too quickly.

<u>Joint Locks</u> - Gyaku Waza

Twin Warrior Capture - Muso Dori

The student starts in a Natural Standing Posture (Shizen No Kamae). The opponent grabs the students right sleeve with his left hand. The student responds by stepping back with the left foot. The students then steps in with the right foot and presses his right open palm under and along the outside of the opponents elbow. The opponents left wrist is caught in the folds of the students right arm. The student then steps back with his right foot whilst pushing on the elbow to straighten it. The students left hand is then used for additional support crossing the arms to twist and apply pressure to the back of the opponents elbow to bring them down to the ground.

<u>Ryusui Iki Nagare</u> - Moving Like Flowing Water

Hand Pillow - Te Makura

The students left hand grabs the opponents right wrist and students right arm hooks up under the opponents upper right arm. The student drops back onto his seat whilst applying an arm bar to pull the attacker forward and down. The student can kick the leg out as he sits down to assist the flow. The student should continue into a roll returning to their feet.

Shoulder Wheel - Kata Guruma

The student is stood in a Natural Standing Posture (Shizen No Kamae). The opponent punches with the right hand (Fudo Ken) towards the students face. The students blocks with a High Block (Jodan Uke) and grabs the opponents right wrist. The students hooks the right arm under the opponents right leg. The student lifts the opponent onto their shoulders and either drops the opponent or drags them over the shoulders to throw them onto their back.

Whirlwind Roll - Uzumaki

The student is stood in a Natural Standing Posture (Shizen No Kamae) The opponent punches with the right hand towards the students face. The student steps back with the left foot and traps the opponents hand against the chest with the left hand. The student brings the right hand in to support the left hand pinning the opponents hand. The student quickly pivots to the left dragging the opponent off balance and throwing them onto their back. Uzumaki means to spin like a whirlwind so you catch the opponents hand and pivot in one swift motion.

Grabbing Forms - Torite Waza

Inside Restraints - Ura Gatame

There are 6 techniques used to restrain the opponent face down on the ground.

1. Restraining the opponent on the ground standing above his right shoulder. This is done by using the left foot to create a step to raise the opponents wrist and applying pressure to the opponents elbow with the right knee.

2. Restraining the opponent on the ground standing below their right shoulder. This is done by using the right foot to create a step to raise the opponents wrist and applying pressure to the opponents elbow with the left

knee.

3. The student extends the opponents right arm out to the side, places the left foot in the opponents armpit and applies Breaking The Bamboo (Take Ori) to the opponents wrist whilst keeping it pinned to the floor.

4. The student moves forwards and applies Twin Warrior Capture (Muso Dori) to the opponents right arm pinning them on the ground.

5. The student turns in trapping the opponents arm against the neck applying Big Twist (O Gyaku).

6. The student lays on the opponents back and hooks both of the arms ready to roll back destorying the shoulders. Do not do the roll!

Outside Restraints - Omote Gatame

There are 6 restraints used to control the opponent face up on the ground.

1. The student places the right foot into the opponents armpit and bends the opponents arm around the right knee in a manner similar to Outside Wrist Twist (Omote Gyaku). You can also use the left leg to brace the opponents arm.

2. The student places the right foot on the opponents neck/face and bends the opponents right arm around the leg.

3. The student places the right foot in the opponents armpit extending the leg and places the opponents outstretched arm on the ground to apply Breaking The Bamboo (Take Ori).

4. The opponent bends his arm and the student follows standing into Kneeling Posture (Suwari Gata) to apply Breaking The Bamboo (Take Ori) pinning the opponents elbow to the floor. Its important to mention that the student uses the legs to pin the opponents arm in position so that he can't slip out of the lock.

5. The student twists the opponents wrist into Outside Wrist Twist (Omote Gyaku).

6. The student performs and Inside Karate Chop (Ura Kiten Ken) to the side of the opponents face and performs a forwards roll (Zenpo Kaiten) to get away from the opponent.

Actual Fighting Training - Shinken Gata Kieko

Give a Ride - Renyo
The opponent steps in with a right punch (Fudo Ken) directed at the students face. The student slides back and to the right with a left inside High Block (Jodan Uke). The opponent then executes a right Front Stamp Kick (Zenpo Geri) and the student moves to the left with the Ninja Walk (Shinobi Aruki) and performs a right outside swinging kick (Sokuyaku Suihei Keri) to the underside of opponents leg. The opponent counters with a grab to the students lapel and the student counters with a right inside Karate Chop (Ura Kiten Ken) to the opponents neck. The student then applies a Inside Wrist Lock (Ura Gyaku) to the opponents right arm while pulling the arm across his stomach for leverage. The opponent resists so the student switches to the Outside Wrist Twist (Omote Gyaku) sweeping the opponents right leg with a Hook Kick (Kagi Keri). It's important to practice flowing with the movements in the form to give a ride (Renyo).

False Space - Koku
The opponent steps in with a right punch (Fudo Ken) directed at the students face, which the student blocks with a High Block (Jodan Uke) followed immediately with an Hammer Fist (Tetsui Fudo Ken) strike to the opponents forearm. The opponent then attacks with a right Forward Stamp Kick (Zenpo Geri) and the student steps to the left to avoid the kick and counters with a right outward swinging kick (Sokuyaku Suihei Keri) to the outside of the opponents kicking leg followed by a left Thumb Drive Fist (Shito Ken) strike to opponents ribs/kidney.

Advanced Attacking Forms - Kogeki Kata

At this point in your training you should be practising at home and looking at how to apply the techniques you have learned so far in a realistic way which means learning to attack. For your Brown Belt grading we want to see 3 advanced level combos demonstrated on the bags, a list of some potential attacking combinations we call the Kogeki Kata (Attacking Forms) can be found on page 19. I have listed some simple combinations for you to practice below:

- Right Front Stamp Kick, Right Reversed Roundhouse, Left Roundhouse, Right Reversed Roundhouse.

- Left High Block, Right Palm Heel Strike, Left Punch, Right Roundhouse, Left Front Stamp Kick.

- Left Front Stamp Kick, Right Roundhouse, Right Reversed Roundhouse, Right Reversed Sweep.

- Left Crushing Block, Right Crushing Block, Right Front Stamp Kick, Left Front Stamp Kick.

Junior Black Belt - 1st Dan

Two Hand Grabs - Ryote Dori
Iron Grip - Kana Shibari
Capture The Demon - Tengu Dori
Two Handed Trap - Ryote Gake

One Hand Grabs - Katate Dori
Place The Throw - Ate Nage
Pulling Drop - Hiki Otoshi
Break And Drop - Setto

Kneeling Forms - Suwari Gata
One Rage - Ichi Geki
Pin Down - Osae Komi
Arm Break - Ude Ori

Defences From Behind - Haibu Yori
Finger Break - Shi Sai
Squeeze The Pulse - Ketsu Myaku

Chokes - Shime Waza
Principle Choke - Hon Jime
Reverse Choke - Gyaku Jime
Painful Choke - Itami Jime
Three Leg Choke - Sankaku Jime
Ear Choke - Mime Jime
Primal Cry Choke - Seion Jime

Practice Forms Of The Escaping Rate - Soto Tonso No Kata
One Hand Escape Form - Kata Ude Tonso No Kata
Left Escape Practice Form - Sayu Tonso No Kata
Rear Grab Escape Practice Form - Kubisuji Tonso No Kata

Two Hand Grabs - Ryote Dori

Iron Grip - Kana Shibari
The opponent grabs the student with both hands at chest height. The student responds by reaching up with both hands over the opponents arms and grabbing onto the opponents collar or shoulders. The student drives two Thumb Knuckle Fists (Koppo Ken) into the pressure points at the side of the neck with pressure. The student then performs a Headbutt (Kikaku Ken) to the opponents nose. The student then steps back and drags the opponent down to the ground whilst applying Iron Grip (Kana Shibari). Alternatively the student can step back with the left foot and twist the opponent down to the ground. You will know if Iron Grip (Kana Shibari) has been done correctly as its very effective.

Capture The Demon - Tengu Dori
This is the counter to Iron Grip (Kana Shibari). The opponent applies Iron Grip (Kana Shibari) to the students neck. The student responds by bringing his arms up and performin a two handed Eight Leaves Strike (Happa Ken) to the opponents ears, The students then grabs the opponents face with both hands and forces the tips of the thumbs into the nostrils or eye sockets. The student then forces the opponents head backwards bringing them off balance and down onto the ground. There is also a one handed variation (Henka) of Capture The Demon (Tengu Dori) in which the student grabs the opponents nose with one hand and then performs a one handed Eight Leaves Strike (Katate Happa Ken) to the bottom of the opponents nose (Jinchu).

Two Handed Trap - Ryote Gake
The opponent grabs the student and applies a double hand grab to the neck. The student responds by dropping the hips

124

while stepping back with the left foot and pushing up on the underside of the opponents elbows. The student then pulls the opponents right arm down whilst lifting the left arm from underneath, Like a wheel. The student then suddenly pivots to the right and kneels down on the right knee while pulling down on the opponents left elbow and pushing up on the opponents right elbow to flip the opponent onto their back in a circular twisting motion.

One Hand Grabs - Katate Dori

Place The Throw - Ate Nage
The opponent grabs the students right lapel with his left hand. The student bends the knees and applies Breaking The Bamboo (Take Ori) while rising with his right hand lifting the opponents arm. The student then punches (Fudo Ken) to the opponents ribs (Butsumetsu) with his left hand. The student then pivots to the right whilse going under the opponents left arm into a position just behind the opponent. The student switches hands so that the left hand is now holding the Breaking The Bamboo lock (Take Ori) on the opponents wrist. The student grabs the opponents left shoulder with his right hand and kicks out the opponents supporting leg to drag him backwards onto the ground. Place The Throw (Ate Nage) should be done in one fluid motion and it's important to use your legs to raise the opponents arm when applying the Breaking The Bamboo wrist lock (Take Ori).

Pulling Drop - Hiki Otoshi
The opponent grabs the student at chest height with the right hand. The student responds by reaching over the back of the opponents hand with the right hand and turns it into Inside Wrist Twist (Ura Gyaku). The student uses the bones in the left wrist to grind into the opponents wrist holding it firmly in place.

The student steps back with the right foot and pulls the opponents wrist towards the right knee throwing the opponent.

Break And Drop - Setto
The opponent grabs the students lapel with the right hand. The student responds by bending the knees and striking to the opponents upper arm (Jakin) with a right punch (Fudo Ken). The student then steps in with the left foot and performs a left punch (Fudo Ken) to the opponents ribs (Butsumetsu) forcing the opponent backwards. The student can step in with the right foot when performing the punch (Fudo Ken) to the upper arm (Jakin) but its important to use the hips and twist to generate momentum. You want to knock the opponents arm upwards releasing the grab.

Kneeling Forms - Suwari Gata

One Rage - Ichi Geki
The student starts in Sitting On One Leg Ready to Stand Posture (Fudoza No Kamae). The opponent grabs the students jacket with his right hand. The student responds by grabbing the opponents arm, leaning back and kicking to the groin (Suzu) with the right foot. After the kick, The student stands up and knocks away the opponents right grabbing hand away with a left Inside Karate Chop (Kiten Ken) to the right wrist. The student then leaps back (Koho Tobi) and assumes a left Number One Posture (Hidari Ichimonji No Kamae).

Pin Down - Osae Komi
The student is in Sitting On One Leg Ready to Stand Posture (Fudoza No Kamae). The opponent grabs the students jacket with his right hand. The student responds by applying an Inside Wrist Twist (Ura Gyaku(to the opponents right arm whilst kicking the opponents raised leg with a right heel shove.

As the opponent goes down, The student uses his left knee on the back of the opponents right elbow to hold him down on his chest continuing to restrain him with the arm lock.

Arm Break - Ude Ori
The student is in Sitting On One Leg Ready to Stand Posture (Fudoza No Kamae). The opponent grabs the students jacket with the left hand and punches with the right hand. The student responds by grabbing the opponents arm, leaning backwards and using his right knee to apply pressure to the back of the opponents straightened left elbow. The student rolls to the left and continues the pressure as an arm lock bringing the opponent face down onto the ground. The student can continue the turn to site upright and apply Breaking The Bamboo (Take Ori).

From Behind - Haibu Yori

Finger Break - Shi Sai
The opponent grabs the back of the students jacket on the right shoulder with the right hand. The student reaches back with his right hand to grab the opponents right hand and then leans forwards slightly to straighten the opponents arm. The student the turns his body to the left and swings his left fist up (Fudo Ken) into the opponents ribs or face. The student then twists the opponents right hand off of his collar with an Inside Wrist Twist (Ura Gyaku). The student then steps back with his left foot using the left hand to apply pressure to the opponents right elbow and applies Breaking The Bamboo (Take Ori) to the wrist. The student then kneels on his left knee to pull the opponent down to restrain him on the ground. The student then kicks the opponent in the chin to force them into submission.

Squeeze The Pulse - Ketsu Myaku
The opponent applies a left rear forearm choke around the students neck (Sankaku Jime). The student responds by bending the knees, raising his shoulders and turning his chin towards the opponents elbow to relieve pressure. The student grabs the choking arm hand with the right hand and applies a single Thumb Drive Fist (Shito Ken) to the bones of the opponents arm with the left hand or applies pressure above the elbow (Radial Nerve). The student hugs the choking arm tightly to the top of his chest and backs out of the choke turning the body. The student passes the opponents left hand from being gripped in the students right hand and the right forearm moves to apply pressure to the opponents left elbow (Ura Gyaku). The student brings the opponent face first down on the ground.

<u>Chokes</u> - Shime Waza

Principle Choke - Hon Jime
The student crosses his wrists and grabs the opponents right lapel with his right hand and his left lapel with his left hand. The students palms face the opponents body and the thumbs are inside the opponents lapels. To apply this choke, The student applies a scissor action with his arms, twisting the knuckles down into the neck.

Reverse Choke - Gyaku Jime
The student crosses his wrists and grabs the opponents right lapel with his right hand and the left lapel with his left hand. The students palms face outwards this time with the fingers inside the opponents lapels. The student applies a scissor like action twisting the knuckles of the hands up into the sides of the neck.

Painful Choke - Itami Jime
The student grabs the opponents lapels straight on with both hands. The right hand to the left lapel and the left hand to the right lapel with the palms of the hands facing down. The student pulls forward while pushing back and inwards with the tips of the extended middle knuckles of the thumbs (Koppo Ken) on both sides of the opponents neck.

Three Leg Choke - Sankaku Jime
From behind the opponent the student reaches around with the left arm and bars his left forearm across the opponents throat. The student then grabs his left wrist with his right hand and pushes into the back of the opponents neck with his forehead. The student applies the choke by lowering his hips while pulling back with the forearm and pushing forwards with his forehead.

Ear Choke - Mime Jime
The student starts in a Natural Standing Posture (Shizen No Kamae). The student reaches up with both hands and grabs the opponents ears. It's important to make sure that you dig your fingernails into the sensitive skin at the back of the ears. The student twists the ears towards the back of the opponents head and pulls the opponent towards him.

Primal Cry Choke - Seion Jime
The student starts in a Natural Standing Posture (Shizen No Kamae). The opponent grabs the students lapel with the right hand. The student responds by supporting the opponents grabbing hand with the left hand, holding it in place. The student then takes a step forwards with the right foot and grabs the opponents throat with the right hand. It's important that the student digs the fingers in behind the windpipe gripping it securely. The student then pulls on the opponents right wrist

and steps back with the left foot to force the opponent backwards with the right hand in a twisting motion, Bringing the opponent down onto his back.

Note: The Primal Cry Choke (Seion Jime) can also be done with a slight sweep with the right foot (Otoshi) if the opponent is resisting.

Practice Forms Of The Escaping Rate - Soto Tonso No Kata

Note from Soke Masaaki Hatsumi (34th Grandmaster)

The following techniques involve the use of Blinding Powder (Metsubishi), Ninja Stars (Shuriken) and camouflage (Goton Po) escape methods of the five elements: Earth, Water, Fire, Wind and Wood. Packets of blinding powder and nine Ninja Stars are concealed in the upper pockets of the jacket (Keogi) and these surprise elements should be combined with the use of body movement (Taijutsu) for the best advantage. To successfully use the strategies of Heaven, Earth and Mankind the Ninja must become one with all things in the universe and embody the spirit of the flowers and bamboo. You must know when to bend with the wind and know when there is no wind to bend to. You must be able to become void itself in order to accomplish your will. If you ask if there is truly such a thing as the fundamental techniques in Ninjutsu, We will say "No". If you ask if you are practising the fundamentals correctly, we will tell you there is no right and wrong way. These movements that we call the fundamentals are only a means for the attainment of the natural ever appropriate responsive movement that comes with personal enlightenment. You need to understand that the journey to black belt (Shodan) is just the start of your training, its certainly not the end.

One Hand Escape Form - Kata Ude Tonso No Kata
The opponent uses his right hand to grab the students right
wrist and pulls the student forwards. The student goes with the
pulling motion making three short shuffling steps forwards. On
the third step, The student lifts his right hand to apply an inside
Breaking The Bamboo (Take Ori) lock to the opponents right
wrist. The student kicks the opponent in the groin (Suzu) with a
right Natural Kick (Sanshin Keri) and steps under the
opponents upheld right arm, turning anti-clockwise and
intensifying the Breaking The Bamboo (Take Ori) wrist fold.
The student applies an Inside Wrist Twist (Ura Gyaku) and
then throws the opponent forwards, scatters blinding powder
(Metsubishi) and escapes by dropping to the ground (You
actually jump in a bush in reality).

Left Escape Practice Form - Sayu Tonso No Kata
The opponent uses his right hand to grab the students left wrist
and pull the student forwards. The student goes with the pull
making three short shuffling steps forwards. On the third step,
The student lifts his left hand to apply an inside Breaking The
Bamboo lock (Take Ori) to the opponents right wrist. The
student then grabs the opponents right shoulder and applies
the Big Twist lock (O Gyaku). The student then does a Natural
Kick (Sanshin Keri) to the opponents groin (Suzu). The student
steps back with his right foot, turning clockwise and pulls
forwards with his right hand while lifting with his left hand to
pull the opponent down to the ground. The student then throws
blinding powder (Metsubishi) in the opponents face and
escapes by dropping to the ground or jumping into a bush.

Rear Grab Escape Practice Form - Kubisuji Tonso No Kata
The opponent grabs the back of the students collar with his
right hand and pulls back. The student goes backwards with
the pull making three shuffling steps while covering the

opponents right hand with his own right hand. On the third move the student uses his right hand to lift and apply a right Inside Wrist Twits (Ura Gyaku(to the opponents right arm while slamming back with a left Elbow Strike (Shuki Ken) to the solar plesxus (Suigetsu).

Note from Sensei Jamie Seal
If you have reached this point in your training you have done extremely well and shown great dedication over the years, Well done!

This will be the hardest grading you have ever done and I'm sure your nervous about doing the test but just remember you have put in a lot of work to get here and know the techniques. I would not let you grade for your black belt unless I truly felt you were ready!

If you don't pass the first time then don't give up, Keep training and try again next month. It's an honour to receive your black belt so it really has to be earned we can't give you any leeway here you have to demonstrate your excellence.

How your black belt grading will work is I will test you on selected techniques from the syllabus and the techniques in the black belt requirements. This will be an extended hour long grading which means we will book you in to do your black belt grading separately at a specifically allocated time so you will have some time to prepare.

Black belt is just the start of the journey there is so much more to study past this and the requirements for the junior black belt dan grades will be set out once you have passed your grading. Good luck!

Upon successfully completing an extended grading and demonstrating that the student has learnt the techniques in the Shadow Warriors Training Manual they will be awarded with their 1st Degree Black Belt and a certificate for their dedication. The student then progresses onto our junior instructors course. If the student is old enough they will progress into the Adult lessons and advanced classes.

Kukishinden Ryu Rokushakubojutsu – Bo Waza and Kamae

Kamae

Jodan No Kamae
Chudan No Kamae
Gedan No Kamae
Tenchijin No Kamae
Hira Ichimonji No Kamae
Ichimonji No Kamae
Seigan no Kamae
Hito No Kamae
Osasaki No Kamae
Chiyoda No Kamae
Kyohen No Kamae

Kukishinden Ryu Bojutsu Wasa

Go Ho
From Hira Ichimonji No Kamae, step back to the left into Ichimonji No Kamae. Perform Bo Furi Gata (3 stage spinning) four times as you step with each strike, on the last step execute an Ashi Barai (leg strike) followed by Kasumi Uchi (temple strike), switch legs and execute a left Ashi Barai, then draw the Bo back throwing it over the head into Ashi Barai, followed by Koho Tobi (backwards leap)

Ura Go Ho
From left Ichimonji No Kamae, perform Bo Furi Gata (3 stage spinning) four times then on the last spin execute a Tsuki, then switch to the left and execute a Kasumi Uchi (temple strike), switch step again into Age Uchi (upwards strike), switch step

134

again into an overhead Kasumi Uchi, followed by Koho Tobi.
*Note: A henka of Ura Go Ho involves the Bo being brought up
with the Age Uchi and the right hand is repositioned to bring
the staff down striking Uke on the top of the head.*

Sashi Al

From left Chudan No Kamae execute a Tsuki, switch legs
stepping through with the right foot into Do Uchi (body strike),
switch step again and perform Age Uchi (upward strike)

Fune Bari

From left Chudan N Kamae, switch step into a right Do Uchi
(body strike) then switch step again into a left Tento Uchi
(Front on middle of the head strike), followed by switching step
into a right Age Uchi, changing leg again into a left Tento Uchi,
followed by Koho Tobi.

Tsuru No Hitoashi

From Hidari Tenchijin No Kamae, Perform Toki Uchi
(downward foot slam with the tip of the Bo), switch step into a
right Ashi Barai, change again into a Left Ashi Barai, followed
by a Huragataman (forward middle of the head strike/flipping
strike without a step), changing again for a right Tento Uchi
and an overhead Ashi Barai

Ura Issoku

From left Gedan No Kamae, change legs into right Ashi Barai,
followed by left Ashi Barai, then Tento Uchi, switch feet again
into right Ashi Barai, then change again into left Ashi Barai,
into Tento Uchi with a Tsuki to end.

Suso Otoshi

From left Chudan No Kamae, switch overhead to perform a Do
Uchi strike, followed by changing step into a left Ashi Barai,

followed by Tento Uchi switching back again for a right Ashi Barai.

Ura Suso Otoshi
From left Chudan No Kamae, Tsuki then switch step into a right Ashi Barai, change again into left Ashi Barai, then again into right Ashi Barai and again into left Ashi Barai followed by Huragataman, then Tsuki with performing Koho Tobi.

Ippon Sugi
From left Tenchijin No Kamae, perform a Toki Uchi, switch legs for a right Ashi Barai, then an overhead Do Uchi, into a rear left Kasumi Uchi, then switch step to perform a left Tento Uchi.

Take Otoshi
From a left Chudan No Kamae, execute a Tsuki then a Kuri Kaeshi (fake Tento Uchi into Hito No Kamae) and then change legs to execute an overhead Kasumi Uchi.

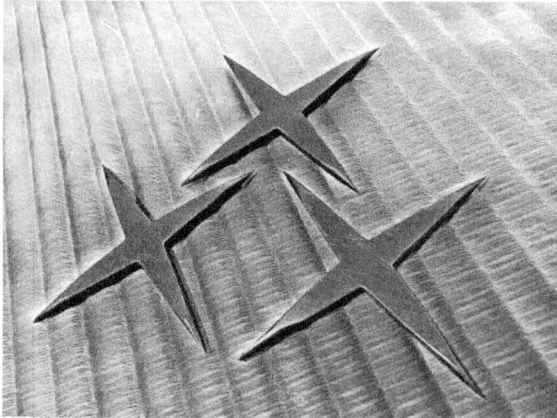

Useful Japanese Words/Phrases

Kukishinden Ryu Rokushakubo Related
Bo Furi Gata - 3 stage spinning
Gyaku Furi - Reversed 3 stage spinning
Ya Dome - Arrow Shield
Hyaku Furi - Spinning horizontally above head
Ashi Barai - Leg Strike
Kasumi Uchi - Temple Strike
Tsuki - Straight Thrust
Age Uchi - Upwards Strike
Do Uchi - Body Strike
Tento Uchi - Front Middle of the head strike
Toki Uchi - Foot Slam
Huragataman - Forward middle of the head/flipping strike without a step
Kuri Kaeshi - Fake Tento Uchi into Hito/Spinning motion bringing the Bo in to and behind the body

Dojo Terminology
Chiko - Walking in Suwari Gata
Migi - Right
Hidari - Left
Omote - Outside
Ura - Inside
Jodan / Ten - High
Chudan / Chi - Middle
Gedan / Jin - Low
Uke - Instigator
Tori - Responder
Ichi - One
Ni - Two
San - Three

Shi - Four
Go - Five
Rokku - Six
Shichi - Seven
Hachi - Eight
Ku - Nine
Ju - Ten
Ju Ichi - Eleven
Ju Ni - Twelve
Ju San - Thirteen
Ju Shi - Fourteen
Ju Go - Fifteen
etc. till: Ni Ju - Twenty, Ni Ju Ichi - Twenty One, Ni Ju Ni - *And so on. 100 being Hyaku, 1000 being Sen.*
Ashi - Leg
Do - Body
Men - Head
Kasumi - Temple
Uko - Neck
Butsumetsu - Chest
Suigetsu - Solar plexus
Kimon - Below the collar bone
Mune - Lapel
Kyoshi/ Kyusho /Kyoshi - pressure point
Kote - Back of hand/wrist
Sabaki Gata - Avoidance
Taisabaki - Footwork
Soke - Grandmaster
Shihan - Master Instructor
Shidoshi - Instructor
Shidoshi Ho - Deputy Instructor
Zen Wan - Forearm
Te - Hand
Sokkotsu - Instep

Koshi - Hip
Jo Wan - Upper Arm
Hiji - Elbow
Benkei - Inside Shin
Wappen - Patch
Hoshi - Star
Mu Kyu - 10th Kyu/Unranked/White Belt - None
Ku Kyu - 9th Kyu - Green Belt -Red & White Wappen
Hachi Kyu - 8th Kyu - Green Belt - Red & White Wappen 1 Silver Hoshi
Nana Kyu - 7th Kyu - Green Belt - Red & White Wappen 2 Silver Hoshi
Rok Kyu - 6th Kyu - Green Belt - Red & White Wappen 3 Silver Hoshi
Go Kyu - 5th Kyu - Green Belt - Red & White Wappen 4 Silver Hoshi
Yon Kyu - 4th Kyu - Green Belt - Red & White Wappen 1 Gold Hoshi
San Kyu - 3rd Kyu - Green Belt - Red & White Wappen 2 Gold Hoshi
Ni Kyu - 2nd Kyu - Green Belt - Red & White Wappen 3 Gold Hoshi
Ikkyu- 1st Kyu - Green Belt - Red & White Wappen 4 Gold Hoshi
Shodan - 1st Dan - Black Belt Red & Black Wappen No Hoshi
NiDan - 2nd Dan - Black Belt Red & Black Wappen 1 Silver Hoshi
Sandan - 3rd Dan - Black Belt Red & Black Wappen 2 Silver Hoshi
Yon Dan - 4th Dan - Black Belt Red & Black Wappen 3 Silver Hoshi
Go Dan - 5th Dan - White/Silver, Red & Black No Hoshi
Rokudan - 6th Dan - White/Silver, Red & Black 1 Gold Hoshi
Nanadan - 7th Dan - White/Silver, Red & Black 2 Gold Hoshi

Budoka - Student

Menkyo Kaiden - license of complete transmission 10th Dan and above

Ryu Ha - School

Bujinkan - Divine Warrior Hall/Palace

Shiken Haramitsu Daikomyo - Ancestral Prayer - *Let every encounter be as beneficial as possible*

Onegaishimas - please assist me

Domo Arigato Gozeimashta - Thank You

Gomenesai - Excuse Me (if bumping into someone)

Sumimasen - Excuse me if asking a question.

Do Itashimaste - Your Welcome

Konbanwa - Good Evening

Oyasuminasai - Good Night/ Sleep Well

Retsuotskute - Line Up

Yamei - Stop

Hajime - Begin

Mo Ichi Do Kutosai - One more time please

Choto Mate Kutosei - Just a moment please

Sensei Ni Rei - Bow to the instructor

Yukuri - Slowly

Daijoubu - are you ok?

Hai - Yes

Iyo - No

Ninpo Ikkan - The spirit of the Ninja is a primary inspiration for us.

Seigan No Kamae / Soshin No Kamae- *Taijutsu* - Ichimonji with rear hand at waist

Nin Gu - Ninja Tools

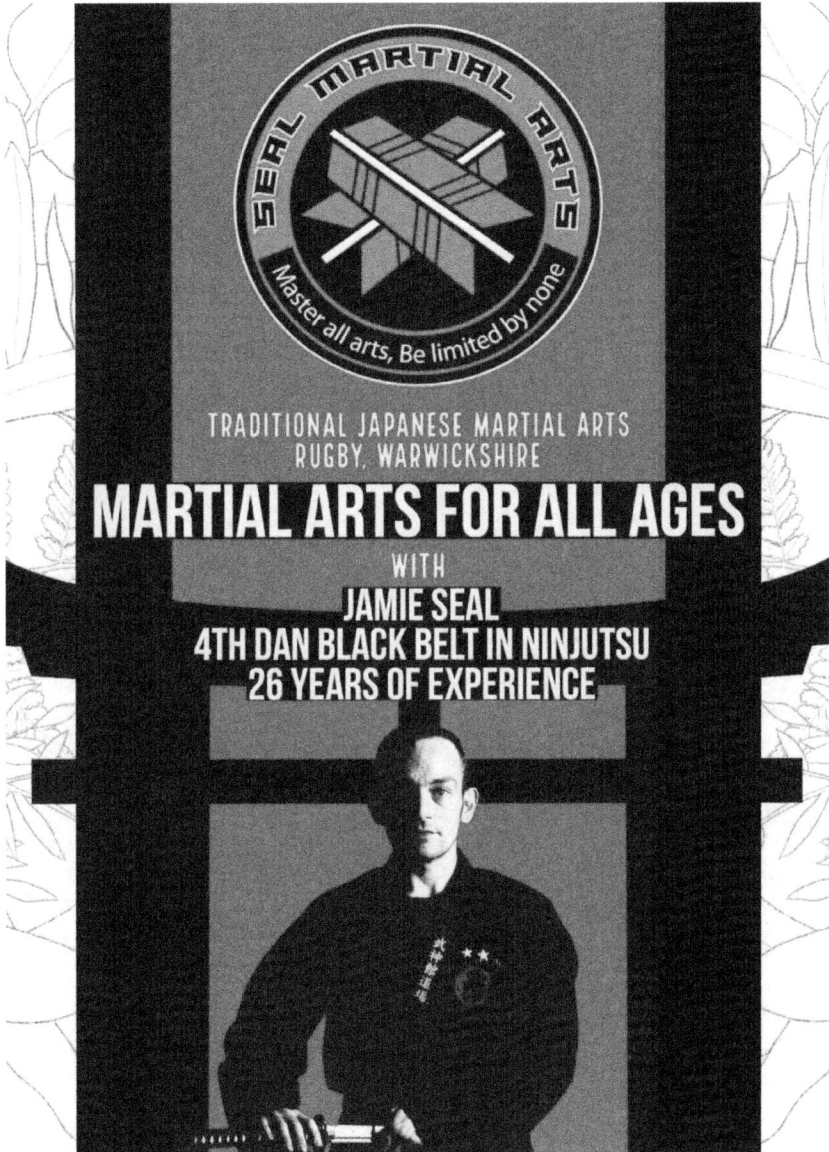

SEAL MARTIAL ARTS

Master all arts, Be limited by none

TRADITIONAL JAPANESE MARTIAL ARTS
RUGBY, WARWICKSHIRE

MARTIAL ARTS FOR ALL AGES
WITH
JAMIE SEAL
4TH DAN BLACK BELT IN NINJUTSU
26 YEARS OF EXPERIENCE

TRADITIONAL JAPANESE MARTIAL ARTS

FOR KIDS & ADULTS

GET IN TOUCH FOR MORE INFO

Printed in Great Britain
by Amazon